G000292500

• Bartholome

WALK SOMERSET & AVON
INCLUDING BATH & BRISTOL

David Perrott and Laurence Main

Bartholomew

A Division of HarperCollins*Publishers*

CONTENTS

Illustrations by Morag Perrott

A catalogue record for this book is available from the British Library.

Published by Bartholomew,
HarperCollins*Publishers*,
77 - 85 Fulham Palace Road, London W6 8JB.

First edition 1993
© Bartholomew 1993

ISBN 0 7028 2177 2

Printed in Great Britain by Bartholomew,
The Edinburgh Press Limited.

Produced for Bartholomew by
Perrott CartoGraphics, Darowen, Machynlleth SY20 8NS.

Typesetting: Perrott CartoGraphics and Litho Link.
Litho origination: Litho Link, Leighton, Welshpool SY21 8HJ.

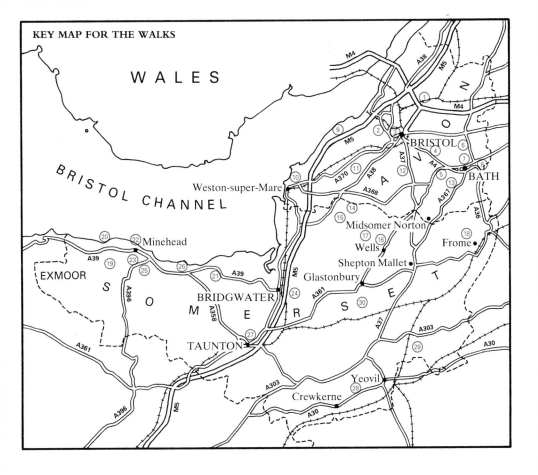

Key to the maps

All maps are drawn on a north axis, ie. with north at the top

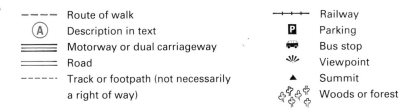

- - - -	Route of walk	—+—+— Railway
Ⓐ	Description in text	🄿 Parking
≡≡≡	Motorway or dual carriageway	🚌 Bus stop
≡≡≡	Road	⅍ Viewpoint
- - - -	Track or footpath (not necessarily a right of way)	▲ Summit
		🌳🌳🌳 Woods or forest

WALKING IN SOMERSET AND AVON

Occupying the southern side of the Severn Estuary, Somerset and Avon include part of Exmoor, The Quantock Hills, The Mendips and the southern extremities of The Cotswolds, making this an area full of potential for the walker. There are also two great cities, linked by the River Avon. Bath with its Roman Baths and elegant Nash terraces, Bristol with its historic docks and fine suspension bridge. Close by, on the coast, the towns of Minehead and Weston-super-Mare are charming traditional resorts.

Many travellers heading for Devon and Cornwall will pass through Somerset without a second thought, yet those who do interrupt their journeys here will be rewarded with countryside that has, quite remarkably, remained free from many of the trappings of tourism.

You can walk some of the ancient paths which William Wordsworth explored in the company of his fellow poet Samuel Taylor Coleridge, and visit the 'mountains green' William Blake had in mind when he wrote of 'those feet in ancient time'.

Walks **19**, **20**, **21**, **22**, **23**, **25** and **26** are all on, or around, Exmoor, and complement those described in another guide in this series, *Walk Exmoor and the Quantocks* by Lyn Rivers.

1 THE LANDSCAPE

Take the train or motorway from the north into Avon and it is hard to tell where Gloucestershire ends and the new county of Avon begins, for both are in the broad valley of the River Severn. Overlooking it, to the east, are the Cotswolds, most walkers' favourite link in the chain of limestone uplands running from Dorset to Lincolnshire.

The western escarpment of the Cotswolds, the part of these famous hills covered by this book, is particularly interesting. Behind it a plateau tilts east, cut by streams and still retaining woods on land that has remained unploughed for centuries.

The Mendips act as a barrier across old Somerset, to the south of Bristol. Climb them to look down on the low, flat, plain of the Somerset Levels, with the Quantocks appearing as the seaward rim. Farmers working the Levels have no need of hedges – they use rhynes (pronounced reens), irrigation channels, to keep their cattle in. Willows line the banks, and underfoot is peat. The Levels were created by waters which have gradually receded from a deep clay basin, and the peat which overlays the clay was formed from decaying plant life. Islands, such as the mystical Glastonbury Tor, are outcrops of the underlying clay and lias. It may come as a surprise to find that there were coal-mines in what is now Avon. The coal deposits are sandwiched between Pennant Sandstone and older Carboniferous Limestone. There is also iron ore under Bristol, where the lower coal measures are covered by clays. The extraction of these minerals gave a basis to local industries, with building stone coming from indigenous Pennant Sandstone and Dolomite Conglomerate.

The fine buildings of Bath were constructed from Cotswold oolite, as were the grassy heights of Cadbury Castle, in the south. Known as Ham stone, it can be seen in churches and houses in Devon.

Ham Hill, near Montacute (Walk **28**), separates the Rivers Yeo and Parrett, which drain into the Levels, with the limestone hills of the Mendips forming a scenic backdrop. Lead was mined here in prehistoric times and was one of the prizes that persuaded the Romans to invade Britain. Lead was still being mined in the Mendips in the early 19th century.

Red sandstone and slate bring a change of scenery in the Quantock Hills. The remote valleys and isolated farms here contrast with the rich farmland of the vale of Taunton Deane, with its apple orchards —'the cider country'.

2 A SHORT HISTORY OF SOMERSET AND AVON

This book covers the territory of the original county of Somerset, with just a small part of old Gloucestershire intruding. The county of Avon was created during the local government reorganisation of 1974, by drawing a new border around Bristol.

Somerset, it has been suggested, was named after a people who came here from Sumeria, and whose capital was at *Somer*ton. The county's name is also linked with the enigmatic landscape feature known as the Glastonbury Zodiac, which can be thought of as a great turning wheel. Zodiac enthusiasts point out that this could explain why an early term for a somersault was a 'somerset'.

Avon takes its name from the River Avon. Avon is the old Celtic word for river, and is an example of the endurance of Celtic names for natural features and places.

Together they occupy a part of the country where myth, legend and history have become intertwined, and archaeological evidence is often difficult to investigate. Even the opportunities for tracing the history of the villages, which may date from at least the Iron Age, are limited due to recent building and development. The caves of the Mendips and the open spaces above them and on the Quantocks and Exmoor have, however, been more revealing. Here the remains of hunters, ancient burial mounds and hillforts have been found.

The stone circles at Stanton Drew, in the lush countryside of the Chew Valley, are the third greatest Stone Age monument in Wessex, after Stonehenge and Avebury. They form a complex pattern of circles, avenues and isolated features, and are quite unusual in that they are located at a low level in rich pastureland. Such monuments were more normally built on chalk downs or moorland.

There were roads in Somerset thousands of years before the Romans came to Britain. The marshy nature of the Somerset Levels made it necessary for the peoples of the New Stone Age to lay down a network of wooden trackways, using hazel, birch and brushwood.

A sophisticated life-style seems to have been pursued during the Iron Age at what were once the lakeside dwellings of Glastonbury and Meare. Existing hillforts were re-occupied and given complicated defences, as at Cadbury Castle, but this did not stop the Romans turning Britain into a province of their empire in AD43. Their local administrative centre seems to have been Ilchester, at the junction of the Fosse Way, with roads from Dorchester and the Polden Hills, where the rich soils could sustain villas. The Romans also left industrial and commercial settlements at Charterhouse and Camerton. Bath became a sacred spa, complete with a temple to Sul Minerva.

Following the withdrawal of the Roman legions, the native Britons, having become used to 400 years of relatively peaceful occupation, were at the mercy of the Teutonic Angle and Saxon tribes, barbarians who lived around the North Sea coast of what is now northern Holland and Germany. They advanced across England, wreaking havoc and plundering as they went, and forcing the civilised and Christianised Britons into Wales and Cornwall. One Celt, Ambrosius Aurelianus, organised an army and made a stand at Badon (somewhere in either Dorset or Wiltshire) at the end of the fifth century. He halted the advance of the English, and the legendary Arthurian period began. The re-occupation of Cadbury Castle around the year 500 gives some credence to the local stories of King Arthur, although firm proof of what really happened at the time is hard to come by. The romantic tales woven around the King and his knights have, however, become part of popular culture, and today sustain a specialist niche in the publishing industry.

At the end of the sixth century Augustine began converting the English to Christianity, and they began to live in peace with their Celtic neighbours. It is interesting to see some of the merging of local place names which resulted from this. For example, a beacon hill near Taunton was called Cructan by the Celts. The Saxons called it beorh (meaning hill). The two were joined to make Crycbeorh, which is now rendered as Creechbarrow.

Somerset became part of the Saxon kingdom of Wessex and was to be the stage for the most dramatic events in the life of its greatest king, Alfred, who burned the famous cakes at Alfred's Burrow, Athelney. This feature of the landscape forms the nose of the Girt Dog of Langport in the Glastonbury Zodiac. An old custom involves the burning of barley cakes, which were then fed to Cerberus, the dog, to gain initiation into the ancient Mysteries.

Alfred turned the tide of war against the Danes, and made them accept Christianity. He baptised their leader in Aller – which appears to be in the middle of nowhere, unless you support the zodiac theory. Alfred chose this spot on the pilgrims' path because it is also on the Girt Dog's back, within the zodiac. He wanted to make Guthrum a fit ruler for the Danelaw by ensuring that he too was initiated into the Mysteries.

Somerset had one more great contribution to make to the mystery and power of the monarchy. When a ceremony was devised for the crowning of Edgar at Bath in 973, it was to last nearly 1000 years and formed the basis of the coronation of Elizabeth II at Westminster Abbey in 1953.

The Middle Ages witnessed the growth of Bristol and the importance of cloth-making to the local economy. This dated from the widespread introduction of fulling mills in the 13th century. Somerset was assessed to pay tax on 601 sacks of wool in 1341, which was more than all the western counties together, with the exception of Wiltshire. Its high price gave it a value comparable to Cotswold wool.

After the turmoil and bloodshed of the 17th century, when Monmouth's rebellious peasant army was routed by James II at Sedgemoor (see Walk **24**), the country was determined to enjoy itself in the settled peace of the 18th century. This was when Bath became the most fashionable place in Britain, under the rule of Richard 'Beau' Nash, whose architectural vision transformed the city.

3 WILDLIFE

The song of the skylark may be heard when walking on the Cotswolds above Bath, with linnets and meadow pipits providing entertainment on the tops of the Mendips. Dense woodland, as at Goblin Combe (Walk **11**) usually has a mixture of broad-leaved trees and conifers. They form habitats for wood pigeons, pheasants, squirrels and green woodpeckers.

Spotted orchis and the spring sandwort are two plants which can survive on the parts of the Mendips that have been worked for lead. Rabbits were once commonly bred on open grasslands and their pelts and flesh formed an important part of the rural economy. Scrubland is bright with ragwort and willowherb, and hedgerows shelter flowers such as red and white campion and navelwort.

The rhynes (drainage ditches) of the Somerset Levels are lined with reeds and sedges, with yellow water iris providing flashes of colour. Dragonflies and waterfowl live in these waterways.

Exmoor's high ground is sparsely covered by heather, but the valleys are lush and green. The bogs and heaths harbour the pale butterwort, a plant covered with sticky glands that catch insects.

4 CLOTHING AND EQUIPMENT

These walks enable you to enjoy walking without having to make an expensive investment in clothing and equipment. Old green lanes and fieldpaths are a fascinating aspect of British walking for the experienced, as well as a gentle introduction for the newcomer. All of these walks can be completed during a dry summer in sensible ordinary shoes, training shoes or wellingtons. If you intend to explore during the winter months, or after prolonged rainfall, you will need a good pair of walking boots.

The south-west of England usually receives a fair amount of rain, so do take a good anorak with you. Waterproof over-trousers are essential in winter. Gloves and a hat, such as a balaclava, are also recommended for winter walking, when spare clothing should also be carried.

A light weight rucksack is ideal for carrying the things you need. A small one will do for a short walk, but it must have room for some food such as dried fruit, nuts or chocolate and a drink. An emergency first-aid kit of patches, antiseptic cream and pain-relieving tablets should be standard equipment, along with a torch and spare batteries. Note that where approximate distances are given, the metric equivalents are also approximate; eg 100 yards or 90 metres.

5 RIGHTS OF WAY

These walks are along established rights of way. Please remember always to keep to the path and regard it as a privilege, as well as a right, to follow them across someone else's land; in that way we can build an atmosphere of co-operation rather than confrontation in the countryside. If you have a dog, please ensure that it does not foul the footpath and *keep it on a lead*. The Animals Act (1971) states that dogs considered to be a danger to livestock may be shot. The Protection of Livestock Act (1953) makes it an offence to permit a dog to worry livestock, with a maximum fine of £200.

Access to the countryside is becoming more and more vital as a means of relaxation in a hectic society. In theory, your rights are well protected by the law but, in practice, some paths become obstructed. Since most people do not like to follow obstructed paths, they become neglected and targets for extinguishment. Please report any obstructions you may find to the local highway authority, which is the respective County Council. For Avon, write to the County Planning Officer, County of Avon, PO Box 46, Middlegate, Whitefriars, Lewins Mead, Bristol, BS99 7EU. Tel. 0272 290777 ext. 318. For Somerset, write to The Director, Rights of Way Section, Environment Dept, Somerset County Council, County Hall, Taunton, TA1 4DY. Tel. 0823 255677.

Obstructions should also be reported to The Ramblers' Association, 1/5 Wandsworth Road, London, SW8 2XX. Tel. 071-582 6878. There are thriving local groups of the Ramblers' Association in both counties. For more information contact: Ms S. Popham, Hon. Secretary, Avon Area of the Ramblers' Association, 56 Falcon Drive, Patchway, Bristol, BS12 5RB and Mr S. Barnard, Hon. Secretary, Somerset Area of the Ramblers' Association, 11 Gordons Close, Taunton, TA1 3DA.

6 THE COUNTRY CODE

Enjoy the countryside and respect its life and work.
Guard against all risk of fire.
Leave gates as you find them.
Keep your dogs under proper control.
Keep to public paths across farmland.
Use gates and stiles to cross fences, hedges and walls.
Leave livestock, crops and machinery alone.
Take your litter home.
Help to keep all water clean.

Protect wildlife, plants and trees.
Take special care on country roads.
Make no unnecessary noise.

7 USEFUL ADDRESSES

Car parking information is given for each walk. British Rail or the West Somerset Railway can also be used to reach the start of several walks. Nearly all can be reached by bus, but please do check these services *before setting out*. Using public transport is the rambler's way of safeguarding the countryside from having yet more roads built. It is also important to support public transport since, for some, it is their only means of access to the countryside. The principal bus company in this area is Badgerline Ltd, Badger House, Old Mixom Crescent, Weston-super-Mare, BS24 9AX. Tel. 0934 416171. Ask about bargain tickets for ramblers, as well as a network map and timetable leaflets. For complete information on buses in the respective counties, contact:
Avon County Council, PO Box 87, Avon House North, St James Barton, Bristol, BS99 7SG. Tel. 0272 557013.
Somerset County Council, County Hall, Taunton, TA1 4DY. Tel. 0823 255696.

There are local *Tourist Information Centres* in many towns and resorts, including:
14 Narrow Quay, Bristol. Tel. 0272 260767.
The Colonnades, Bath. Tel. 0225 462831.
Town Hall, Market Place, Wells. Tel. 0749 672552.
The Library, Corporation Street, Taunton. Tel. 0823 274785.
Market House, The Parade, Minehead. Tel. 0643 702624.
Beach Lawns, Weston-super-Mare. Tel. 0934 626838.
They all provide information on accommodation, events, attractions and entertainments.
The relevant Weathercall telephone forecast for this area is on 0839 500405.

THE FROME VALLEY

7 miles (11.3 km) Easy

Follow delightful riverside paths past tranquil meadows. These are linked to form a signposted route known as the Frome Valley Walkway, which leads under a spectacular railway viaduct.

2 *Pass Brook Farm on your right. Take its access track to a lane. Go right to the B4058 road. Go left for 30 yards (25 m) and turn right through a small wooden gate to follow a path diagonally across a field. Take a kissing-gate in the wall ahead and bear right along the edge of this field to a road. Go right along the road and fork left with the signposted Frome Valley Walkway. Cross the River Frome and turn left to walk upstream. Bear left over a foot-bridge and turn right to keep walking upstream along a walled path. Maintain this direction along a lane (The Dingle). Turn right to cross Damsons Bridge. Turn left to walk upstream with the Frome on your left. Cross a foot-bridge and turn right under a railway viaduct.*

3 *Walk with the Frome on your right to a foot-bridge. Cross it and turn left. When you reach a concrete farm bridge, do not cross it. Go on to a second (stone) bridge, near a signpost. Turn right, away from it, along a hedged track. When this becomes a metalled lane, turn right along an enclosed path. Cross one road to go between garden fences to a second. Turn right for 50 yards (45m).*

4 *Turn left along Heather Avenue for 250 yards (230 m). Bear right over a stile and cross the corner of a field. Turn right, cross a stile in the far fence and follow the path which leads under the railway to the A432. Go right along the pavement, pass Park Lane, then turn right at Down Road. Turn left along Bury Hill. Fork right and take the signposted path ahead in the next corner. Return to a road, go right and descend to go straight ahead to a crossroads, and cross over.*

1 *Start from Hambrook Post Office, near the north-eastern edge of Bristol. Park at the roadside, or come on the X29 bus.*
With your back to the Post Office, go left to take a signposted path. Reach a roundabout on your left. Turn right along an enclosed path.

5 *Bear left to walk with the Frome on your right. Fork right to cross the river. Turn left along the Frome Valley Walkway. Go left at a lane to cross the river and turn right just before Rock Cottage. This path leads back to the B4058. Go left back to Hambrook Post Office.*

A The Dingle was settled by coal-miners in the 19th century.

B Bury Hillfort dates from 700BC. Its ramparts are well-preserved, except on the western side. It was adapted and used by the Romans.

0   1 mile

0   1 km

On this walk you can admire spectacular scenery at the very edge of Bristol. A woodland path leads to the dramatic limestone gorge which is spanned by the famous Clifton Suspension Bridge.

5 *Reach the edge of the wood. Turn left along a path which keeps just inside it. Go ahead through a gap in a wall to reach the open space with cottages again. Bear right to retrace your steps to the start.*

4 *Turn left under a high, open arch. Follow the woodland path, keeping straight on when a fork bears right. Climb to another junction and go right to a firm track. Turn left along this.*

3 *Bear right, then almost immediately fork right again. Reach a stone wall and take the narrow path on your right. A steep descent leads to the Avon Walkway. This is a firm track running beside the river.*

Turn left to walk with the Avon on your right. Gated archways under an old railway appear on your left. Follow this track for 1 mile (1.6 km).

2 *Bear left at the initial fork. Come to an open space with cottages away to your left. Bear right to enter Stokeleigh Camp. Go ahead to a viewpoint over the gorge, with the bridge on your right. Turn left and follow the path as it bears right out of the Iron Age hillfort, reaching a pond on your left.*

1 *Start from Clifton, on the west side of Bristol. Buses, including nos 8 and 9 from Bristol Temple Meads station, stop near the junction of Clifton Down Road and The Promenade. Follow the B3129 to Clifton* *Suspension Bridge. Cross it and go sharp right along North Road. Follow the pavement to a stile on your right. Turn right over it into the woodland of the Avon Gorge National Nature Reserve.*

River Avon

Avon Gorge

Avon Gorge Nature Reserve

Stokeleigh Camp

B

C

Clifton Suspension Bridge

A

B3129

A Clifton Suspension Bridge was finished in 1864, after the death of its designer, Brunel.

B Stokeleigh Camp guarded an old ford here around 250BC. It now occupies a corner of the nature reserve.

C This is the course of the dismantled railway between Bristol and Portishead.

BRISTOL

5 miles (8 km) Moderate

Bristol Docks enter the heart of the city, giving this walk a maritime theme. Turn inland to see St Mary Redcliffe, which Elizabeth I described in 1574 as 'the fairest, goodliest and most famous parish church in England'. The quaint and well worn 17th-century Christmas Steps lead to views from Brandon Hill.

A The Arnolfini Gallery is housed in Bush House, which was built in the 1830s as a tea warehouse. Major exhibitions of contemporary art are held here. *Open Mon-Sat 10am-7pm, Sun noon-7pm.*

B Bristol Industrial Museum occupies a disused transit shed in the City Docks. Its fascinating collection portrays the variety of work done in Bristol since the establishment of a port, and the growth of a soap industry, in the late 12th century. These domestic industries continued for many years, with Bristol soap being sold to the woollen mills of Gloucestershire. When John Cabot sailed from here to Newfoundland in 1497, the city's trade was given an international dimension. By the 18th century it was the most important city in England after London. Wealth came from the triangular trade of sending finished goods to Africa, slaves from there to the West Indies, and sugar, rum, spices and tobacco back to Bristol. At one time the city was famous for its chocolate. By 1900 heavier industries based on iron and steel were predominant. The clothing industry was the chief employer until the 1920s, when light engineering, the aircraft industry and road vehicle building became important. The River Avon was canalised in the early 19th century to create the City Docks. New docks at Avonmouth and Portishead were built as the size of ships increased in the late 19th century. A new container terminal and deep-water dock was built at Portbury in the 1970s. *The Industrial Museum is open Sat-Wed 10am-1pm; 2-5pm.*

C The Heritage Centre displays Bristol's rich shipbuilding heritage. *Open daily 10am-6pm (5pm in winter).* Nearby is the famous *S.S. Great Britain.* Designed by Brunel and launched in Bristol on 19th July 1843, she was the first propeller-driven, ocean-going, iron ship to be built. She carried thousands of passengers to America and Australia and served as a troopship in the Crimean War and the Indian Mutiny. In 1861 she took the first-ever English cricket team to visit Australia. From 1882 she served as a cargo sailing ship, carrying South Wales coal to San Francisco and returning with wheat. Both voyages were by way of Cape Horn. Returning to Cardiff in 1886, she was forced to shelter at Port Stanley in the Falkland Islands. She was never to sail again. Used as a store for coal and wool, she was beached in Sparrow Cove when made redundant in 1937. In 1970 she was salvaged and brought back for display and restoration in Bristol. Entrance is by token, which can be purchased at the Maritime Heritage Centre.

D The church of St Mary Redcliffe is a fine example of 15th-century perpendicular architecture.

E The Exploratory is an exciting place for budding scientists. *Open daily 10am-5pm.* Admission charge.

F St John's Gate dates from the Middle Ages. Notice the statues of Brennus and Belinus, the legendary founders of Bristol.

G Red Lodge has splendid 16th-century oak panelling. *Open Mon-Sat 10am-1pm; 2-5pm.* Admission charge.

H The City Museum and Art Gallery has a particularly interesting collection of Bristol blue glass. *Open daily 10am-5pm.*

I Cabot Tower was built in 1897, 400 years after John Cabot's ships from Bristol discovered the mainland of North America. Some say the new continent was named after Richard a'Meryk (from the Welsh ap Meurig), the collector of customs who paid Cabot his 'king's reward'.

J The Georgian House was built as the town house of a sugar merchant. *Open Mon-Sat 10am-1pm; 2pm-5pm.*

K Bristol Cathedral was created in 1542 out of the former Abbey of St Augustine. Augustine was a missionary from Rome who met the long-established Celtic Christians here in 603.

Over

0   1 mile

0   1 km

6   *Turn left at the top of the steps to notice the 15th-century almshouses and chapel on your left. Take the zebra crossing to go up Lower Park Row. This climbs to the 16th-century Red Lodge. Continue along Park Row. Cross at the lights to the University Tower. Next door is the City Museum and Art Gallery. Go ahead to the next pelican crossing and turn left across both roads. Go ahead to Berkeley Square. Follow the pavement to its far corner. Go through to Brandon Hill and climb with the path on your right to the Cabot Tower.*

7   *Pass the tower on your left and descend Brandon Hill to the gates of Great George Street. Turn left through them and pass The Georgian House (no 7) on your right. Reach Park Street and turn right down to College Green. Cross this to the cathedral. Turn left down to the statue of Neptune which presides over St Augustine's Reach. Turn right along Narrow Quay to follow the waterfront back to the Tourist Information Centre, on your left.*

5   *Bear left into Castle Park and follow a path to Newgate. Go left uphill as the road changes name to Wine Street. Turn right at the top, down Broad Street. Go through St John's Gate at the bottom. Turn right to see St John's Conduit, then turn left, then right along Christmas Street. Go ahead across a road (Lewins Mead). Turn left to pass St Bartholomew's Hospital. Turn right up Christmas Steps.*

1   *Start from the Tourist Information Centre at 14 Narrow Quay, Bristol. There is a car park nearby, in Prince Street. If you arrive by train at Bristol Temple Meads Station, join this route at point no **4**.*
Go left to pass the Arnolfini Gallery. Turn right across Prince Street swing bridge. Go right along the waterfront, with the Floating Harbour on your right. Pass the Bristol Industrial Museum on your left. Continue to the Maritime Heritage Centre and S.S. Great Britain.

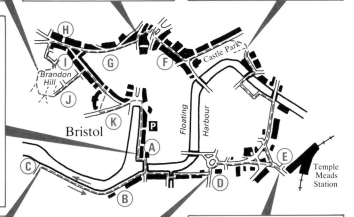

2   *Retrace your steps along the waterfront to Prince Street swing bridge. Do NOT cross it! Go ahead over Wapping Road and along Merchants Quay. Take the bridge across the access channel to Bathurst Basin (on your right). Go left to pass the Ostrich Inn on your right. Bear right up steps to Redcliffe Parade East. Go left along this road towards St Mary Redcliffe Church.*

3   *Cross the road to St Mary Redcliffe Church. Go left, then right, to pass it on your right. Keep to the right of a flyover. Cross Temple Gate to The Exploratory, at the foot of the approach to Temple Meads Station.*

4   *With your back to The Exploratory, go right and bear right along Temple Way. Approach a bridge and fork right down steps to the waterfront. Turn left to go under the bridge, with the Floating Harbour on your right. Follow the path as it turns left to a road (Temple Back). Go right, then turn right over a bridge to Passage Street. Turn left along Queen Street and bear right into Castle Street.*

Walk 4

BITTON STEAM CENTRE

8 miles (12.9 km) Easy

Level walking with fine views is provided by the elevated course of a dismantled railway from Bitton to Bath. If you come on a day when trains are running on the Avon Valley Railway, you can combine this walk with a ride. Tel: (0272) 327296 for timetable information.

A Keynsham once had an Augustinian abbey, founded in 1170. It was later a centre of the brass industry and is now a suburb of Bristol. The name Keynsham is derived from St Keyne, one of the 24 daughters of King Brychan of Brecon, who achieved sainthood around 500. She fled here from unwelcome suitors.

B The Dramway Footpath follows the route taken by an old horse-drawn tramway, constructed around 1830 to take coal from Coalpit Heath to the River Avon.

C The Midland Railway opened this through route from Bath to Gloucester via Mangotsfield in 1869. Closed in 1971, steam trains run at times on the preserved Avon Valley Railway from Bitton Station.

D The course of the dismantled railway to Bath is now a cycle way.

E St Mary's Church dates from Saxon times. Roundheads damaged it in 1643.

F Brunel's Great Western Railway between London and Bristol opened in 1841.

G The Avon Walkway runs from Pill to Dundas Aqueduct.

Bitton Steam Railway

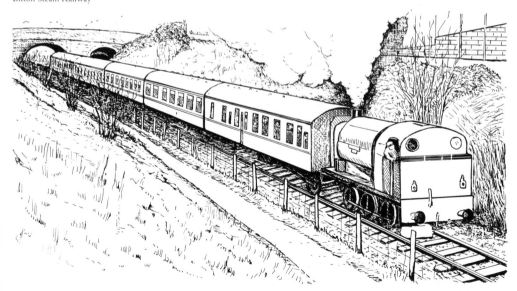

Over

0   1 mile

0   1 km

2   *Turn right just before a small stone bridge across a tributary. A signpost marks the Dramway Footpath. Take the concrete lane past Londonderry Farm on your right. Go left along the A4175 for 250 yards (230m). Bear right up a signposted public footpath which soon bears left to pass through a garden centre and reach the A431.*

3   *Turn right to go under an old railway bridge. Turn left up to the Avon Valley Railway at Bitton Station. Go left along the cycle way on the disused railway.*

4   *Cross the River Avon. Continue to cross a bridge over a road. Turn right down steps to the road and go left to pass the Bird in Hand pub on your left. Pass St Mary's church, Saltford, tucked away on your right. Pass Beech Road on your left. Take Norman Road ahead for 30 yards (25 m), then turn right along a walled track. This crosses over a railway tunnel and bears left above the railway on your left. Go ahead to a waymark post in the corner of the third field. Take the gap ahead and turn right along a hedged path. Emerge in a field and follow the hedge on your right. Turn left in the corner.*

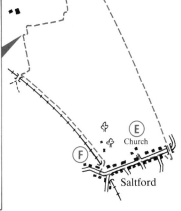

Ⓒ Bitton Steam Centre

A431

Ⓑ Londonderry Farm

A4175

Ⓓ

A4175

Keynsham

River Avon

Avon Walkway

Ⓖ

Station Ⓐ P

Ⓔ Church

Ⓕ

Saltford

1   *Start from the British Rail Station at Keynsham, between Bath and Bristol. Leave from the northern side, where you would alight from Bristol. The car park is here.*
Go right along the A4175. Ignore Avon Mill Lane crossing a bridge on your right. Go ahead into the Borough of Kingswood and over bridges across two channels of the River Avon. Turn right along a road to the old bridge near the Lock Keeper pub. Turn right along the signposted public footpath to Willsbridge. This goes under the A4175's bridge and passes a lock on your left. Pass Cadbury's chocolate factory across the river.

5   *Go right, as waymarked, in the next corner, and turn left for 20 yards (18m). Turn right, beside a hedge on your right, to another corner. Go left for 100 yards (90m), turn right over a foot-bridge and go left in the next field. Turn right in the field corner to reach a stile on your left. Cross it, bear right to the railway viaduct and go right to take a stile back onto the cycle way on your left. Go left to cross the river again, then turn left down steps. Follow the Avon Walkway, with the river on your left, back to the Lock Keeper pub. Retrace your steps to Keynsham Station.*

Walk 5
NEWTON ST LOE

6 miles (9.7 km) Moderate

The crest of a low hill hides the delightful village of Newton St Loe from the gaze of commuters on the A4 or the railway between Bath and Bristol. Here is an older world with a slower pace and one of the finest estates in the area. The towpath of the River Avon brings added peace to this relaxing walk.

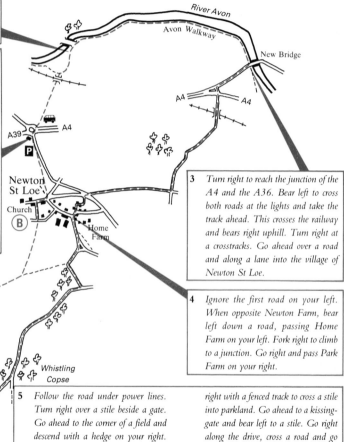

2 *Turn right to walk with the Avon on your left. Go under an old railway bridge and continue to a road bridge. Climb up to the A4 road.*

1 *Start from the Globe Inn, near the junction of the A4 and the A39 between Bath and Saltford. There is roadside parking here. There is a bus stop nearby for nos X3, X38, X39 and 339 between Bath and Bristol. With your back to the pub, go ahead across the road, passing a roundabout on your left. Turn left across the A4, passing the bus stops on your right. Take the signposted public footpath ahead. Go over a stile in the wall, cross a track and continue over a stile in a hedge. Take a tunnel under the railway to reach the River Avon.*

3 *Turn right to reach the junction of the A4 and the A36. Bear left to cross both roads at the lights and take the track ahead. This crosses the railway and bears right uphill. Turn right at a crosstracks. Go ahead over a road and along a lane into the village of Newton St Loe.*

4 *Ignore the first road on your left. When opposite Newton Farm, bear left down a road, passing Home Farm on your left. Fork right to climb to a junction. Go right and pass Park Farm on your right.*

5 *Follow the road under power lines. Turn right over a stile beside a gate. Go ahead to the corner of a field and descend with a hedge on your right. Continue over a stile and pass woodland on your right. Reach playing-fields and bear right to a lane. This turns left through a gate. Turn right with a fenced track to cross a stile into parkland. Go ahead to a kissing-gate and bear left to a stile. Go right along the drive, cross a road and go uphill to pass the church on your left. Go right, then left to take a kissing-gate and go down the right-hand edge of a field back to the Globe Inn.*

A Bath College of Higher Education now occupies the Georgian mansion of Newton Park. Prince Charles is the landlord and sometimes visits.

B Holy Trinity Church, Newton St Loe, has two charming old sun dials.

Walk 6
LANSDOWN
6 miles (9.7 km) Moderate

This splendid downland walk above Bath provides superb views towards Bristol and the Mendips and allows you to set foot on Bath Race Course, the site of an important Civil War battle. It has been a venue for flat racing since 1830; there are now ten days racing each year.

5 Turn left at a path junction. Go to the end of the wood on your right. Bear left down to a gate. Do not go through it!

Beach Wood

Cotswold Way

Monument

C

4 Join a track and bear right along it. Go through a gate to pass a golf course on your right. Fork right at the corner of the wood on your left.

Pipley Wood

Golf course

B

A

Little Down Hillfort

Bath Racecourse

Lansdown

Prospect Stile

6 Go right through a gap in the wall and follow the wall on your left. Cross a stile, go ahead to the summit of Hanging Hill. Take the stile near it and turn right. Go through a gate and pass a radio mast on your right to reach a lane. Follow the signposted Cotswold Way to a road. Cross it to take a stile and bear left to the Lansdown Monument. Pass it on your left. Cross a stile and follow a wall on your left to a stone stile ahead.

7 Cross the stile and leave the Cotswold Way by turning right. Go through a gate, over a stile and bear right. Go ahead through two gates. After a third, near a barn, turn half-right to a stile between a building and some trees. Go ahead to the main road and turn left along it to return to the Park and Ride bus terminus, on your right.

3 Do not cross the stile! Turn right to follow a fence on your left. Go ahead over a stile and reach a hill fort in the next corner. Go right along its rampart. Turn left through a way-marked gap to cross its interior and leave by a stile beside a gate. Descend to a waymark post and turn sharply right to reach a stile beside a gate.

2 Face the pub and go left to step over a rail in a gap in the wall. Go ahead to the race course and turn right to walk between it on your left and a wall on your right. Continue behind the grandstands of Bath Race Course, then bear left to cross the course. Go ahead 50 yards (45m) and turn half right to cross the course again at its bend, pass the end of a straight section of railing and reach a topograph in the far corner, above Prospect Stile.

1 Start from the Park and Ride bus terminus, Lansdown, which is to the north of Bath. There is a bus service (no 31) on weekdays from Bath (Queen Square). Cross the road from the terminus and turn left to follow a narrow metalled path beside it. Cross the road to reach the Blathwayt Arms on your left.

A Little Down Iron Age hillfort was a promontory fort, with a ditch only on the Lansdown Plateau side.

B The Cotswold Way runs for nearly 100 miles (161 km) between Bath and Chipping Campden.

C The monument is to Sir Bevill Grenville, leader of the Cornish Royalists at the battle, in 1643.

15

REGENCY BATH

3 miles (4.8 km) Easy

This walk takes you past the graceful buildings erected for the upper classes who flocked to Bath in the 18th century. Queen Anne's visit in 1702 made the spa fashionable, while 'Beau' Nash turned the place into a holiday resort for the fashionable. The towpath of the River Avon offers tranquility.

5   *Turn left up Marlborough Buildings. Turn right to follow Royal Crescent and Brock Street to The Circus. Bear slightly left to take Bennett Street past the Assembly Rooms and Costume Museum on your right. Turn left up Russell Street and bear right across Julian Road to visit the Industrial Heritage Centre. With your back to the Centre, go left along the raised pavement of Julian Road. Cross Lansdown Road and go down Guinea Lane.*

6   *Cross the road at a junction to no 33 Paragon, where the actress Sarah Siddons (1755-1831) lived. Turn right along the pavement. Pass the Building of Bath Museum and the Museum of English Naive Art on your right, then no 1 Paragon, where Jane Austen stayed, on your left. Turn right along George Street, then left down Milsom Street. Bear left into New Bond Street and turn right down New Bond Street Place. Continue down Union Passage and across Cheap Street to Abbey Church-yard. Go right to retrace your steps along York Street to the Roman Baths and the Tourist Information Centre.*

1   *Follow signs to the Tourist Information Centre in the middle of Bath. If arriving at the railway or bus stations, walk north through the shopping centre. There are well signposted car parks.*

Facing the Tourist Information Centre, go right, then left under the Colonnades of Bath Street to the Pump Room and Roman Baths. Go right and turn left along York Street. Turn right into Abbey Green and turn left along North Parade Passage, passing Sally Lunn's House on your left. Go ahead along North Parade and cross a bridge over the River Avon.

2   *Turn left down a spiral staircase housed in a turret of the bridge to reach the river towpath. Go left to pass under the bridge and follow the river on your right. Continue under a railway bridge, then over a canal bridge. Follow the signposted Avon Walkway under a foot-bridge and another railway bridge. Turn right across a wide bridge for pedestrians.*

Victoria Park

Bath

River Avon

Station

P

A36

4   *Pass under a third bridge, used by pedestrians. Turn right immediately to go up steps to it. Turn left to reach Bristol Road (A4) and go ahead across this (there is a pelican crossing nearby on your right). Turn left along its pavement, then turn right at a fenced path up to Royal Victoria Park. Turn right to pass the Victoria Column.*

3   *Turn left to walk with the river on your left. Pass Churchill Bridge on your left, following the towpath under two road bridges.*

A Bath's most famous attraction is the Roman Baths. The hot springs were discovered by Bladud, the father of King Lear. One story tells how he suffered from leprosy and was condemned to exile as a shepherd. Pigs led him to the medicinal mud which cured his leprosy. The Romans developed the springs and named the place Aqua Sulis. This honoured the Celtic deity Sul, linked with the Roman goddess Minerva. When the Romans left, the springs continued to flow into reservoirs built by them. The baths continued to be visited, and in the early 18th century Bath was becoming a highly fashionable spa. Large-scale rebuilding resulted in the

Over

REGENCY BATH
Continued

discovery of the Roman Baths. They are *open daily 9am-6pm Mar-Oct (plus 8-10pm Aug), 9am (Sun 10am)-5pm Nov-Feb*. A combined ticket can be bought to include admission to the Museum of Costume and Assembly Rooms (see **G**).

B Sally Lunn's Refreshments House and Museum is probably the oldest house in Bath, perhaps dating from 1482. Excavations have revealed Roman, Saxon and Medieval buildings here. Sally Lunn was a Huguenot refugee who baked buns from 1680. Her buns became famous and the secret recipe is still followed. *Open daily except Christmas and New Year, 10am-5pm (noon-6pm Sun)*. Admission charge.

C North Parade was where William Wordsworth stayed in 1841 – but most probably at no 12 – not at no 9 which has the commemorative plaque.

D Victoria Park was opened by Princess Victoria in 1830, when she was 11 years old. She didn't enjoy her visit, which is commemorated by the Victoria Column, and never returned to the city.

E Royal Crescent is a magnificent curving terrrace of 30 houses, built 1767 to 1775, and designed as one harmonious whole, with rows of Ionic columns supporting a continuous frieze. It was part of John Wood the Elder's plan, but his son John Wood the Younger actually designed it. Mrs Montagu lived at no 16 and became 18th-century Bath's most celebrated

Royal Crescent

hostess. Known as the 'Queen of the Bluestockings', she held parties where intellectual conversations were preferred to the more usual gambling. No 11 has romantic connections. Elizabeth Linley, the beautiful singer, eloped from it with her future husband, the playwright Richard Sheridan. The 'Grand Old Duke of York' of the nursery rhyme (George III's son) lived at no 1. Today, this house is preserved and open to the public, *Apr-Sep daily 11am-5pm, Mar and Oct-mid Dec Tues-Sun 11am-4pm*. Admission charge.

F The Circus is a beautiful sweep of terraces, completed by Wood the Younger after his father's death in 1754. William Pitt the Elder lived at no 7 and served as Bath's MP from 1757 to 1766.

G A large and prestigious collection of fashionable 16th to 20th century dress for men, women and children, displayed in the famous 18th-century Assembly Rooms. *Open Mar-Oct daily 9am (Sun 10am)-6pm, Nov-Feb 10am*

(Sun 11am)-5pm. A combined ticket is available for this and the Roman Baths (see **A**).

H The Industrial Heritage Centre tells the fascinating story of a family firm, dealing in mineral water. *Open Easter-Oct daily plus winter weekends 10am-5pm*.

I No 1 Paragon is where Jane Austen stayed on her early visits to Bath. It was the home of her uncle James Leigh Perrot and his wife, who invited the Austens to stay with them whilst they hunted for a house of their own. Across the road is the Building of Bath Museum, with a fabulous city model. *Open mid Jan-mid Dec Thurs-Sat 10am-5pm, Sun-Tues 2-5pm, Wed 10am-noon*. Next door is the Museum of English Naive Art, celebrating folk painting. *Open March-Christmas daily 10.30pm-5pm (Sun 2-6pm)*. Admission charge.

J Milsom Street was frequented by Anne Elliot and Captain Wentworth in Jane Austen's novel *Persuasion*.

BATH ABBEY

6 miles (9.7 km) Strenuous

Follow the footsteps of Jane Austen around Bath and view the city from the surrounding hills. Relax on the towpath of the Kennet and Avon Canal and discover how easy it is to escape the busy city streets yet still be near the centre. Connections with famous people abound in the elegant terraces.

A Bath Abbey was rebuilt by Oliver King, the Bishop of Bath and Wells appointed by Henry VII, whom he served as secretary. The Norman Abbey was badly in need of repair in 1499 when the bishop dreamt of a ladder between heaven and earth, complete with angelic host. An olive tree and a crown were also featured. The connection was made by a voice saying, 'Let an *Olive* establish the crown and let a *King* restore the church.' The olive tree and crown are carved in stone on the buttresses on either side of the West Front. A statue of Henry VII appears over the West Door. The abbey is dedicated to SS Peter and Paul, whose statues are on each side of the door. The actual door was given by the brother of Bishop Montegue in the 17th century and bears the Montegue and Tudor coats of arms.

The present abbey occupies only the site of its predecessor's nave, although the Norman cathedral was never completed. It was the Normans who moved the bishopric from Wells to Bath, where the Saxons had an abbey. A 12th-century bishop preferred Wells and ruled that the bishop should have a throne in both places. The present bishop has his only throne in Wells now, but retains Bath in his title. The Saxon abbey was where Edgar, the first king of all England, was crowned in 973.

B The High Street is where the poet Samuel Taylor Coleridge lodged at the Greyhound in December 1813. He suffered a physical and mental crisis, induced by opium.

C Laura Place is where Jane Austen wrote in *Persuasion* that Lady Dalrymple and her daughter 'would be living in style'.

D Henrietta Park has a scented garden for the blind.

E The classical elegance of Great Pulteney Street is where Catherine Morland and the Allens had lodgings in Jane Austen's *Northanger Abbey*. Emma Hamilton, Lord Nelson's mistress, is known to have stayed at nos 12 and 72, as well as nearby at no 6 Edward Street. Louis XVII of France also lived at no 72 Great Pulteney Street during his exile in 1813. When Napoleon III was deposed by the French in 1871, he too came to this street, staying at no 55. Ironically, two great British admirals who defeated the French off Ushant in 1794 lived here - Admiral Howe at no 71 and Admiral Hood at no 34.

F Jane Austen lived at 4 Sydney Place, from 1801 to 1804. In between working on *Northanger Abbey* and nursing her sick parents, Jane went across the road to Sydney Gardens. Sydney House or Tavern, with its ballroom, is now the Holburne Museum and Crafts Study Centre. *Open from mid Feb to mid Dec, Mon-Sat 11am-5pm, Sun 2.30-6pm. No 93*

Sydney Place was where Charlotte, George III's queen, stayed in 1817. Her son the Duke of Clarence, and future King William IV stayed nearby at no 103. The royal party did not stay long, having to return to Windsor for a funeral.

G Jane Austen was living in Bath when the Kennet and Avon Canal was being dug between Newbury and Bath. This created an inland navigation link between London and Bristol, with the aid of the rivers Thames, Kennet and Avon. It was opened in 1810. The canal is 57 miles long and is of exceptionally high architectural quality. The entry into Bath is particularly impressive. Widcombe Locks, a flight of six, takes the canal down to join the Avon. With the building of the nearby railway, trade on the canal dwindled to nothing, and it was closed in 1951. In 1990 it was reopened to through navigation by the K & A Canal Society and British Waterways, although water supplies are too precarious for parts of the canal to operate in dry weather.

H Jane Austen's characters walked along the top of Beechen Cliff, 'That noble hill whose beautiful verdure and hanging coppice render it so striking an object from almost every opening in Bath'.

Over

1 Bath is well served by trains and buses. There are several signposted car parks. Look for signs pointing to the Tourist Information Centre at the Colonnades.

Go left from the Tourist Information Centre to the Roman Baths. Go right, then left to Bath Abbey. Bear left up High Street. Turn right across Pulteney Bridge. Go left at Laura Place and enter Henrietta Park on your right. Exit on your right and go up to Great Pulteney Street. Turn left for the Holburne Museum. Pass it on your left to bear left into Sydney Gardens. Go right towards the railway, cross it by the second bridge and go across the canal to reach Sydney Road. Turn left and left again at Beckford Road.

2 Turn right to follow the canal towpath. Pass a wooden foot-bridge on your right, then cross the next, stone bridge. Continue to Bathampton Lane and go right.

3 Bear left across Warminster Road and go up a track. Cross a stile and bear right along a path which climbs above the trees.

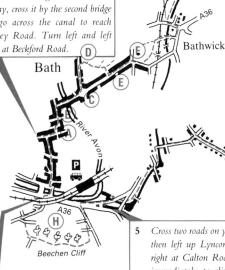

4 Go right along a track which passes a golf clubhouse and a sham castle on your left. Cross a stile and bear left beside a fence to a foot-bridge taking you to Bath University. Go ahead to the Computer Centre, turn right to Bathwick Hill and bear right down it. Turn left opposite Cleveland Walk, bear right down a path to the canal. Go left along its towpath. When it joins the Avon, bear left up the pavement.

5 Cross two roads on your left, go right then left up Lyncombe Hill. Turn right at Calton Road and turn left immediately to climb steps. Bear right along Beechen Cliff, passing Alexandra Park on your left. Continue to steep steps on your right. Go down them and bear left to Holloway. Turn right downhill and when the road bears right, go straight ahead down a paved path.

6 Reach Wells Road, go right to take a subway under it and continue under the railway. Take the pedestrian bridge over the Avon. Go ahead up Southgate and Stall Street back to the Roman Baths. Turn left to return to the Tourist Information Centre.

REDCLIFF BAY

5.5 miles (8.9 km) Moderate

South Wales and the town of Newport are the backdrop to the sweeping view across the Severn Estuary from these clifftops, where the south-westerly winds blowing up the Bristol Channel have bent trees across the path. Inland the tranquil scenery and woods shelter an old church with a memorial to a Prime Minister.

2 *Pass Newhaven Road on your right. Turn left into Waterside Park. Go straight ahead, towards the sea, along a path between two houses. Descend to the coast path. Turn left along it, above the sea on your right. After 1 mile (1.6 km) turn left through a small wooden gate into a caravan park.*

1 *Start from the terminus for buses to Portishead from Bristol (nos 358, 359, 658 & 659). This is near the top of Nove Road, Redcliff Bay. Considerate roadside parking is possible lower down.*
Go to the junction at the top of Nove Road and turn right along Down Road. Reach a public footpath signpost on your right. Turn right down this path. Go left when it reaches a road. Turn sharply right at a road junction, then go left along Hillside Road.

3 *Follow the public footpath uphill through the caravan park. Bear right at the top to reach Down Road. Turn right and follow it as it bends left. Look out for a 'Road Narrows' sign on your right. Take the signposted public footpath on your left at this point.*

Redcliff Bay

Charlecombe Wood

BRISTOL CHANNEL

Walton Bay

Weston Wood

B3124

Church Weston in Gordano

Down Farm

Common Hill Wood

Hack's Wood

5 *Reach a waymark post at a T junction. Turn right along a track which descends to a stile. Cross it and turn left to walk with woods on your left and along the tops of two fields on your right. Turn right in the corner of the second field and descend to a road. Go left to St Peter and St Paul's church in Weston in Gordano. Continue to the White Hart pub.*

6 *Turn left along Hill Lane, opposite the White Hart. Continue along the signposted footpath at the end of this lane. Climb to where the fenced corner of a field appears on your right. Keep climbing to an old green lane. Pass a stile in the hedge on your right. Go ahead along Valley Road. Turn right at its bottom to return to the start.*

4 *Climb through woodland to downland. Join a grassy track. Continue along a track through Common Hill Wood.*

A Walton Common Down is rich in ancient earthworks.

B The cross in the churchyard of SS Peter and Paul is a memorial to the only British Prime Minister to have been assassinated. Spencer Perceval was shot dead in 1812, by a merchant who had been bankrupted.

Walk 10
WESTON-SUPER-MARE
5 miles (8 km) Moderate

Weston-super-Mare's sandy beach is a glorious sight, but only at high tide. The Bristol Channel acts as a funnel to produce the second highest tidal range in the world, of over 40 feet (12.5 m), leaving a wide expanse of mud flats in this shallow bay at low tide. Starting from the Tropicana Pleasure Beach, this walk climbs up to an Iron Age Hillfort overlooking the resort.

Sand Bay

Birnbeck Island

Spring Cove

Worlebury Hill

Worlebury Hillfort

C

3 *Turn left to climb steps up the hill to a small open space. Turn right along the ridgeway path through the woods.*

Anchor Head

2 *Go left, then bear right at the top of Madeira Road. Turn right at the top to follow South Road. Pass Camp Road on your left. Turn left up Trinity Road. Turn right at its top to follow a path into woodland.*

Knightstone

B

Weston-super-Mare

1 *Start from the Tropicana Pleasure Beach, on the seafront at Weston-super-Mare. This resort is well served by buses and trains.*
Go left to follow Marine Parade. Pass the Grand Pier, the causeway to Knightstone and the marine lake. Follow the prom at Madeira Cove to pass under the pavilion, then fork right up to Birnbeck Road.

Grand Pier

Weston Bay

A370

P

A

4 *Ignore signposted paths on both sides. Pass a reservoir and water tower on your left. Reach a signposted path junction. Bear left along the bridleway to Kewstoke. Ignore the faint path going left through the trees after 100 yards (90 m). Go ahead another 50 yards (45 m) to a signpost. Turn left along a public bridleway. Ignore all side paths and descend gradually to a flight of stone steps on your left. This is part of a waymarked footpath which crosses your track. Turn left up these steps to return through Worlebury Hillfort to your outward path. Go right along it back to the open space. Turn left to retrace your steps back into Weston-super-Mare.*

A The Tropicana Pleasure Beach has a heated pool with a wave machine, together with the usual water chutes. For model railway enthusiasts there is an extensive layout complete with 30 trains, representing all periods and settings. Tropicana is visited by Super Ted and is *open daily from 10am between May and September.* Admission charge.

B Knightstone was an island until the causeway was constructed. An elegant Bath House, built here in 1831, was scorned by the Rev Francis Kilvert, who visited in 1872. He preferred the 'delicious feeling of freedom in stripping in the open air and running down naked to the sea, where the waves were curling white with foam and the red morning sunshine glowing upon the naked limbs of the bathers'. He died aged 32.

C Trees planted in 1923 hide the ramparts and tumbled stone walls of Worlebury Hillfort. Hundreds of people lived here in the late Iron Age around 300BC. Later, the Romans were probably responsible for butchering the inhabitants, who may have been of the Dobunni tribe. Their wealth probably came from the lead trade. There is archaeological evidence that the hillfort was revived around AD500.

Walk 11

GOBLIN COMBE

4 miles (6.4 km) Easy, but muddy in wet weather

This is a splendid walk through a narrow valley, where a cloak of trees increases the sense of remoteness. It is possible to park a car in Wrington and make this a circular walk of 7 miles (11.3 km) by following the road back from Cleeve. Public transport allows a linear walk to be enjoyed, however, using buses from Bristol or Weston-super-Mare. The two villages are on different routes between these two centres, so it makes sense to buy a day rambler ticket.

4 Go ahead over a cross track, which curves away to your left and then to your right.
Continue along the valley track through the gap in a wall ahead. Pass the limestone crags on your right. Keep left at a fork to reach Walnut Tree Farm's access lane. Go ahead 30 yards (25 m), then turn right along an enclosed path.

5 Continue across a field to a road. Turn left to cross Cleeve Hill Road and reach the Lord Nelson pub. Return to either Bristol or Weston-super-Mare on bus nos 351, 352 or 353. If you are walking back to a parked car in Wrington, take Cleeve Hill Road (an extra 3 miles or 4.8 km).

3 When the metalled road bears right to Barley Farm, go straight ahead up the hedged track to Meeting House Farm. Bear left and descend past woodland on your left. Look for the end of the field on your right, go ahead 50 yards (45 m) and turn left down a public footpath through the woods. This soon bears right and keeps to the valley bottom.

1 Start from Wrington Post Office. Bus nos 820 and 821 from Bristol or Weston-super-Mare stop here, and there is easy roadside parking.
With your back to Wrington Post Office, go left along Broad Street. Turn left at Silver Street and almost immediately right along School Road.

2 Go ahead over Long Lane and up Old Hill (a No Through Road signposted as a public bridleway).

A It is hard to believe, but Bristol Airport is only 1 mile (1.6 km) east of here.

B Limestone cliffs rise above the trees in Goblin Combe. Birch, oak and beech provide shelter for squirrels. The goblins seem to have disappeared, replaced these days by rock climbers and weekend walkers.

Walk 12

STANTON DREW

4 miles (6.4 km) Easy

0 _____ 1 mile
0 _____ 1 km

Stanton Drew has three stone circles, one of which is particularly large. Tradition states that they were formed when dancers at a wedding were turned into stone for extending their frolics from Saturday night to Sunday morning. This walk visits the two best stone circles and continues to Hauteville's Quoit. This is said to have been thrown from Maes Knoll by Sir John Hauteville in the 13th century. The Great Circle and the South West Circle (unvisited on this walk) align with it.

5 *Ignore the gate on your right immediately after the bridge, then turn right through the next gate. Walk along a narrow meadow and through a gate, then bear left towards a bend in the river. Turn left over a stile and follow the river round on your right to Byemills Farm's access lane. Go left up it and turn right over a stile near a gate. Go ahead to another stile beside a gate.*

6 *Cross the narrow field to a stile ahead. Continue beside a fence on your right. Take a stile in the corner and bear right to cross a stile and meadows, to a track in the far right corner. This leads under the old railway viaduct to a road in Pensford. Turn right to pass the Rising Sun pub on your right, followed by the disused All Saints Church. Cross the bridge and go left back to the bus stops or your car.*

1 *Pensford, where this walk starts, is 5 miles (8 km) south of Bristol. Cars may be parked considerably in the village, and bus no 376 between Bristol and Yeovil stops here.*
Walk from the bridge which carries the A37 over the River Chew to the war memorial. Turn right, then turn left, following the signposted Avon cycle way, away from another bridge. Turn right again to pass the old church, which is across the river on your right.

2 *Take the first field gate on your right. Walk towards the old railway viaduct and pass under it near the river on your right. Continue through a gate (with a Two Rivers Way symbol on it) in the far corner of this long meadow. Bear slightly right to a stile in the hedge ahead. Cross it and follow the fence on your right to a stile in the next corner. Continue over it and towards a building (Bye Mills). Take the gate to pass this on your right and go ahead over a stile in the far hedge, bear slightly left to cross a foot-bridge and follow the left hand edge of a meadow. Cross a stile in the corner and walk with a hedge on your right.*

3 *Cross a road to take the gate opposite. Bear right to cross the corner of a field to a gateway leading back to the road. Cross this to enter the field opposite. Follow a track through a waymarked gap to reach a stile in a hedge at the end of a market garden. Go ahead to a gate in the far right corner of the next field. Continue to a stile beside another gate. Follow a track with a hedge on your right, go over a stile and take the track into Stanton Drew.*

4 *Turn sharply right along the access lane to visit the stone circles. Retrace your steps and go right along the road through the village. Cross the medieval bridge and follow the pavement to the B3130. Turn right along this road and pass Hauteville Quoit Farm on your right. Follow the road over a bridge.*

A Pensford Railway viaduct was opened in 1873. The line (between Bristol and Radstock) closed, together with the last local coal mine, in 1973.

B Stanton Drew stone circles are some of the most fascinating late Neolithic monuments. They may have replaced earlier timber structures around 2000BC. The Great Circle of 27 stones (originally perhaps 30) has a diameter of 123 yards (112.4 m).

PRISTON MILL

4 miles (6.4 km) Moderate

Undulating hills just to the west of Bath offer splendid views over rolling farmland, where wild flowers grow in abundance beneath the hedgerows of wide tracks. The focus of this walk is an old mill which still grinds flour. Look out for a mysterious earthwork, the Wansdyke.

7 *Turn right along the road and soon ignore a track bearing right. Go ahead along the road for over 1 mile (1.6 km), passing Pennsylvania Farm on your left. When the road next bears left, go straight ahead along a hedged path. Cross a stream by a bridge, bear right over a stile and follow a fieldpath up to a gate. Continue past a pond on your left and take a gate to reach the lane opposite the churchyard steps.*

1 *Start from St Peter's Church, Englishcombe. This village is about 1 mile (1.6 km) along a lane from the south-western edge of Bath. Cars may be parked considerately in the village. If you come by public transport, take bus no 10 or 11 from Bath's bus station to Southdown (not Sun).*

Alight at Padleigh Turn and walk down Padleigh Hill, and then along Englishcombe Road.
Go down steps at the side of the churchyard and turn left along a lane. Reach Manor Farm and turn right along a No Through Road.

2 *Continue along a rough track. When it bears left to a fieldgate, go down the narrow hedged path ahead.*

3 *Cross a foot-bridge over a stream and climb to a road at Inglesbatch. Bear right and then turn right near the telephone box down a No Through Road.*

4 *Facing Home Farm, turn right down a track which is signposted as Mill Lane. Continue through a gate, along a little more track and through a fieldgate ahead. Follow telephone poles across the field and take a stile on your right. Bear left to cross a foot-bridge over a stream. Go ahead towards Priston Mill.*

6 *Go ahead to a stile in the fence ahead. Cross it and bear slightly right down to a foot-bridge. Cross this and go up the next field towards Wilmington. Go ahead over two stiles to reach a road.*

5 *Walk through the mill and turn right at the car park. Do not bear right with the concrete lane. Go ahead along a grassy track. Take the first gate and climb to go through a second.*

A Faint traces of an earthwork can be seen in this field. It is part of the Wansdyke.

B Wholemeal flour is still ground at Priston, a water mill built in the 18th century. Milling was first recorded here in 931. *Open Easter-Sep daily 2.15-5pm (11am-5.30pm Sat & Sun)*. Admission charge.

Walk 14

ROCK OF AGES

3.5 miles (5.6 km) Moderate

A limestone gorge with a famous rock provides the focus for this ramble over the Mendips. Most of the high ground is heath, covered by bracken. There are magnificent views in all directions and woodland adds variety. Butterflies, dragonflies and damselflies abound in summer.

1 *Start from the public car park south of The Burrington pub, beside the B3134 road, 2 miles (3.2 km) west of Blagdon. There is a scenic summer special bus service, no 819, to Burrington Turn from Bath or Weston-super-Mare, between late May and late September (weekdays only). Otherwise take the no 674 bus (on weekdays only) from Bristol to Blagdon.*
Turn right along the B3134 to pass the pub and garden centre. Cross the road carefully and bear left up a No Through Road after a post box. This climbs and becomes a track. Pass a house on your right and reach a gate on your right.

7 *Cross the road carefully and take the track going left from a car park. Ignore paths going left and right, then fork left. A narrow path joins from your right. Bear right at a fork ahead. Descend through woodland to a roughly surfaced lane. Go left along it. Pass the turning for Burrington Church on your right. Go ahead to the B3134. Turn left and walk back to the car park past the garden centre and pub on your left. The Rock of Ages is opposite, beside the B3134.*

2 *Turn left, away from the gate, to take a track across the heath. After 400 yards (365 m), turn left at a crosstracks. Pass a turning on your right after 20 yards (18 m) then ignore a path bearing left. Go ahead along the well-trodden path down to West Twin Brook.*

3 *Cross the brook and bear left. Follow this path to East Twin Brook.*

4 *Cross the brook in its steep-sided valley. Follow the path which goes left to climb out of the valley. Walk for nearly 1 mile (1.6 km) past heath on your right and fields on your left.*

5 *When other paths converge on yours from the right, follow it as it bears left. Descend between fields to pass Ellick House on your left.*

6 *Go left down the B3134 road for 100 yards (90 m).*

A 'Rock of ages, cleft for me,
Let me hide myself in Thee'
are the first lines of the well-known hymn composed by Augustus Toplady. A curate from nearby Blagdon, he was inspired to verse when forced to shelter in the deep cleft down the middle of this massive rock during a storm in the 18th century.

B East Twin Brook disappears into a swallet. A typical feature of the limestone Mendips, a swallet is where a stream runs underground.

CHEDDAR

5 miles (8 km) Strenuous

0 ⊢——————————————————— 1 mile

0 ⊢——————————————————— 1 km

Cheddar Gorge justly deserves all the superlatives used to describe it. This walk takes you around its rim and through a Nature Reserve. The views of the reservoir, the Mendips and over the Somerset Levels are superb, and there are also splendid sights underground – so allow time to visit the caves after this walk.

6 Go ahead along the path which crosses a stile, and a field, to a gate ahead. Go through this and walk with a wall on your right. Cross a stile beside a gate in the corner, then continue downhill on a grassy path, with Cheddar Reservoir ahead. Take a stile in the wall on your left. Go through woodland and turn right through a kissing-gate in the wall. Turn left downhill.

5 Leave the West Mendip Way by turning left when the path reaches a farm track. Cross the cattle grid and go ahead to a farm.

4 Emerge over a stile beside a gate and follow a fence which becomes a wall on your left. Go ahead over one stile in a fence and encounter two more stiles which have lost their fences.

West Mendip Way

D

7 Reach houses and turn sharply left along a narrow path with a wall on your right. Reach a broad track and bear left with it down to the B3135 road. Go right to return to the car park.

Cheddar Cliffs

B

B3135

C

A

Cheddar Gorge

Cheddar

P

Gough's Cave

Jacob's Ladder

3 Go straight across the road and take a kissing-gate beside a gate opposite. Go ahead along the track which is waymarked 'Shipham 5 miles'. Ignore sidepaths into the woods. Pass old limekilns on your left. Walk with a wall on your right and cliffs on your left. Ignore a stone stile between two gates on your right. Swing left with the main track to cross a stile beside a gate to enter woodland. Bear left at a fork.

2 Turn left off the road and soon bear left along a path which goes uphill. Pass Prospect Tower and climb to the top of Cheddar Gorge. Join the waymarked West Mendip Way and descend with it through woodland. The path swings right, to reach the B3135 road.

1 Start from the public car park in Cheddar, next to the hotel. The entrance to Jacob's Ladder is across the road. Cheddar is on the A371 between Weston-super-Mare and Wells. Bus nos 126 and 826 provide a good daily service from these two towns.

From the car park, go right along the B3135 to a road junction. Turn left and fork left uphill.

Over

A Cheddar's deep limestone gorge is one of the most dramatic sights in England. It was probably cut thousands of years ago by a river, which now takes an underground route to emerge near the start of this walk. The sheer walls of rock shelter rare plants, such as the Cheddar Pink, but you must go underground for the most spectacular treasures. Two of the hundreds of caves are open to the public. Gough's Cave is where the skeleton of a man dated to about 7000BC was discovered in 1903. Cox's Cave was opened up in 1837. Ponds reflect the displays of stalagmites and stalactites and a museum houses the many finds. *Open daily except Christmas, 10am-5.30pm Easter-Sep, 10.30am-4.30pm Oct-Easter.* Admission charge. A flight of 322 steps known as Jacob's Ladder leads to Prospect Tower and provides a short cut on this route, if you are prepared to pay the admission fee. Local strawberries are well worth buying on a summer's day, and, of course, the place is famous for cheese. The Saxon King Edmund was almost carried over the edge of the gorge by his horse when out hunting in 941. Samuel Taylor Coleridge also walked in this area, and there are some who link the gorge and caves with the lines in his poem *Kubla Khan:*
'In Xanadu did Kubla Khan
A stately pleasure-dome decree:
Where Alph, the sacred river, ran
Through caverns measureless to man
Down to a sunless sea.'

B The public footpath which winds along the top of the gorge forms part of the Bristol Countryway. This 81 mile (130.5 km) route goes from Slimbridge to Weston-super-Mare, via Bath.

C Black Rock Nature Reserve has mixed woodland and rough downland.Here you may well see yellowhammers, and common spotted and greater butterfly orchids.

D The West Mendip Way is a splendid 30 mile (48.5 km) route between Wells and Uphill. It was devised and waymarked by Rotary Clubs to commemorate Queen Elizabeth II's Silver Jubilee in 1977.

Cheddar Gorge

WELLS

6.5 miles (10.5 km) Strenuous

Breathtaking views over Ebbor Gorge are rivalled by the splendour of Wells Cathedral on this bracing walk.

Hidden away, but within easy reach, are the caves at Wookey Hole. Legend has it that a witch used to live here, until a monk poured holy water over her, turning her to stone. It is an enchanting place.

A Wells Cathedral is the favourite of many, ranking with Durham and Salisbury for its architecture. Edward the Elder decided that this should be the cathedral city for Somerset and the first bishop was consecrated here in 909. After the Norman Conquest, the first Norman bishop decided to move to Bath, destroying the canonical buildings at Wells. Bishop Robert of Lewes (1136-66) preferred to restore Wells, whilst retaining Bath. He had two thrones and laid down that chapters in both places should elect future bishops. As if this wasn't complicated enough, Bishop Savaric (1192-1205) coveted the abbey at Glastonbury. He obtained it and became Bishop of Bath and Glastonbury. His successor gave up the abbacy in 1219 and was simply Bishop of Bath. The pope had to enforce the agreement whereby the chapter of Wells had to be consulted after Bishop Roger was voted in by the monks of Bath alone in 1244. He became the Bishop of Bath and Wells and this title has been kept by all his successors. Since the dissolution of Bath Abbey in 1539, the bishop has been voted for by the chapter of Wells only. The cathedral we see today, with its magnificent West Front, was begun around 1180. The central tower was raised to its present height about 1320 and the ingenious inverted arches were inserted around 1340. They transfer the weight from west to east, brace the supports of the tower and widen the foundations. There is a 14th-century clock.

B Divert from this route along a beautiful wooded valley to see Wookey Hole Caves. These were carved out by the underground River Axe, which emerges from the north of the caves to provide water power for riverside mills. Men and women were living in these caves 30,000 years ago, and people still found shelter here in Roman times, and more recently. Human bones, a dagger and significantly, an alabaster ball of about the right period lend credence to the legend of the witch. Take a trip down Hell's Ladder to the Witch's Kitchen and you'll see the stalagmite that is presumed to be her. Modern legends are being created by the divers who explore further into the cave system at great personal risk.

Emerging into the light, you can visit the paper mill. It has served as such since at least 1610. The Domesday Book of 1086 records a corn mill and the site may also have been used for fulling cloth during the Middle Ages. A good supply of clean water, drying breezes and lack of air pollution, combined with proximity to Bristol and Wells from where cotton rags could be obtained, made it the ideal place for a paper mill. Machines took over the making of paper in the 19th century, but handmade paper still continued to be preferred for legal documents and watermarked bank notes. Commercial production did not finish until 1972. The process was revived in 1976 by Madame Tussaud's, who also store wax heads here. You can also see a fairground collection. The whole complex is *open daily 9.30am-5.30pm in the summer, 10.30am-4.30pm in the winter.* Admission charge.

C Ebbor Gorge Nature Reserve is deeply wooded. The valley was carved out by an ancient river and the sides are high limestone cliffs. A beautiful place, it was donated to the National Trust in 1967 by Mrs Olive Hodgkinson, in memory of Sir Winston Churchill. It is managed by the Nature Conservancy Council as an unspoilt habitat, where buzzards nest and badgers dig their setts. Voles, moles, weasels, stoats, rabbits, grey squirrels and foxes live here, as do deer. Hawthorn, ash, oak, hazel and elder form the bulk of the trees. Avoid treading on birdsfoot trefoil, dog's mercury, traveller's joy, yellow archangel, wood sorrel, bluebells and marsh marigolds. Green and great spotted woodpecker, sparrowhawk, kestrel, linnet, jay, stonechat, blackcap, woodcock, owl, goldcrest and bats are all present.

Over

6 Reach the road sign for Wookey Hole and turn right through the waymarked gate. Follow an enclosed path to a fork. Bear left along the lower path. Go ahead over a stile beside a gate to enter Ebbor Gorge National Nature Reserve. Follow the valley track for 200 yards (185 m), then fork right up steps along the waymarked path for Priddy. Divert left at the top to the viewpoint, then resume your former direction.

7 Go ahead at a crosspaths. Climb to cross a stile beside a gate. Continue over a higher stile and follow a fence on your left. Pass a stile on your left. Keep beside a wall on your left, ignoring another stile in it. Take a gap ahead and ignore a gate on your left.

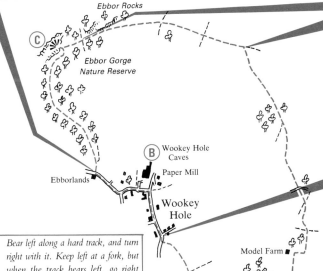

8 Take the gate ahead in the corner, then bear right to a gate in the hedge. Descend to a field where you bear slightly left to a waymarked gate. Go down to a lane and cross a stone stile on its far side. Go left to cross a stile in the hedge and go right along a farm track back to Wells, retracing your steps from the junction near the quarry.

5 Pass Milton Lane on your right and follow the road as it bears left past School Hill, the Paper Mill and the access lane to Wookey Hole Caves on your right. Ignore a lane on your left. Bear right with the road towards Cheddar.

4 Bear left along a hard track, and turn right with it. Keep left at a fork, but when the track bears left, go right through a waymarked gate into a field. Go ahead to go through a kissing-gate. Take a fenced path to Wookey Hole. Go right along Coombe Brook.

2 Turn left along a lane waymarked as the West Mendip Way. Turn right with it, then immediately turn left along Lovers Walk to pass playing fields on your right. Turn right at a junction and continue past schools to a road.

3 Turn left for 10 yards (9 m), then turn right across the road and take the narrow waymarked path up steps ahead. Cross a higher road to join a lane, which passes a quarry on your left.

1 Start from the Tourist Information Centre in the Market Place, Wells. This is down the High Street from the bus station (where buses come from all directions), and car park. Take Sadler Street out of the Market Place, and pass the gateway to Cathedral Green and the West Front of Wells Cathedral on your right. Bear right along New Street.

4 miles (6.4 km) Easy

Priddy is situated in a shallow hollow about 1000 feet (305 m) above sea level in the Mendips. It has been the venue of an August fair ever since 1348, when the black death engulfed the cities and it could no longer be held in Wells. Perhaps the fair recalled older occasions. In local legend Jesus came here with his great-uncle Joseph of Arimathea, a tin-trader. 'As sure as the Lord was at Priddy' is a local saying. The name Priddy means 'earth' in the sense of 'world'. 'Pryd' in Welsh means 'the beauty of Natural Order', or 'As Above, So Below'. William Blake had the Somerset legends in mind when he wrote:
'And did those feet in ancient time walk upon England's mountains green and was the Holy Lamb of God on England's pleasant pastures seen?'.

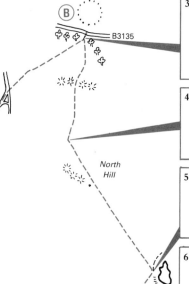

2 *When Nine Barrows Lane bends left and an old drove road (waymarked with a red arrow for a by-way) goes right, take a waymarked gate into the field ahead. Bear left to a metal gate in its far corner.*

B3135

Nine Barrows Lane

Greenhill

■ Church

Ⓐ

Ⓟ

Priddy

Wells Road

North Hill

Ⓑ

Underbarrow Farm

St Cuthbert's Swallet

Ⓒ

3 *The Priddy Circles are on private land, across the B3135 road from the metal gate. With your back to the road and gate, go straight ahead up the field to the Priddy Nine Barrows. Continue to more barrows on the top of the hill.*

4 *Take a small, waymarked, wooden gate, or cross the stile beside it. Go ahead beside a wall on your right. Continue over a stile and keep the wall on your right.*

5 *With Mineries Pool ahead of you, turn right to pass the old lead works on your left. Bear right with the path to cross a lane, then bear left to rejoin it and go ahead to reach a road.*

6 *Turn right to follow this road back to Priddy. Pass East Water Lane on your right. Reach a T junction and turn right back to the New Inn, on your left.*

right to follow a hedge on your right to a gate out of the churchyard. Go ahead over a field to take the gate opposite and reach a road. This is Nine Barrows Lane. Turn right along it. Pass Priddy Pool on your left.

1 *Priddy is 4 miles (6.4 km) north of Wells. It has no public transport, but there is plenty of space to park a car. With your back to the New Inn, start by taking the second road on your left.*

Pass the triangular village green on your left. Fork right up to St Laurence's church. Pass it on your

A St Laurence's church, Priddy, contains an 11th-century font and a 15th-century tapestry and rood screens. When a visiting preacher tried to use the pulpit the clerk told him 'Plaze Zur, we doo ut all down here, and (the farmer's) goose be sitting on twelve aggs and she won't hatch this vortnight'.

B Four mysterious circles lie in the fields north of the B3135. They date from the Bronze Age.

C St Cuthbert's Lead Works closed in 1908. Priddy had been a producer of this valuable metal since prehistoric and Roman times.

MELLS

4 miles (6.4 km) Moderate

Little Jack Horner really did pull out a plum when he acquired the deeds of the manor house at Mells, during the Dissolution. It had belonged to Glastonbury Abbey, for whom John Horner worked as a bailiff. This was an industrial centre between 1744 and 1844 but nature has returned in triumph, covering the ruined mills in Wadbury Valley with trees.

1 *Start from Mells Post Office, which is 3 miles (4.8 km) west of Frome. The no 184 bus (Frome to Bath) stops here.*
Face the Post Office and go right. Fork left along the road signposted for Great Elm. Go ahead 300 yards (275 m), then turn right along a track. This follows Wadbury Valley. Walk above Mells Stream on your right.

2 *Bear left at a fork to pass above an old lock and weir on your right. The ruins of an old iron works lie near the stream. Continue beside a wall on your right, then above the stream again. Pass the garden gate of 'Greenleaves' on your left.*

3 *Fork right to leave the track and follow the waymarked Wyvern Way. Keep near the stream, go ahead over a stile and pass through a plantation of conifer trees. Bear left, away from the stream.*

7 *As the road approaches a T junction, go ahead over a stile and turn left over the grass. Pass a gate on your right, go ahead to a stile in the hedge and turn right over it. Cross a road to take a stile a little to your right. Descend to a footpath sign, turn right and reach a stile in the hedge on your left. Take it to descend to the bottom corner. Cross a stile in it and take the road ahead over a bridge to return to the post office.*

6 *Go right along the road. Pass the entrance of a quarry on your left, with others on your right. When you pass a second quarry entrance on your left, go ahead 100 yards (90 m) and look for a waymark post for a 'perimeter path' on your left. Turn left over a stile and turn right immediately to take this path. It runs parallel to the road on your right.*

5 *Do not continue over a stile in the corner of the field, but turn right along a tree-lined track. At its end, turn left over a stile and turn right to follow the right hand edge of this field. Continue over stiles to reach a road.*

4 *Cross a stone stile beside a gate ahead. Reach a road in Great Elm and continue downhill. Turn right to cross Mells Stream. Turn right across the stile beside a gate. Immediately turn left up a narrow path between the trees, ignoring the track going ahead on the floor of this valley. Bear right at the top. Emerge at a road. Go left, then right, over a stile to take a track.*

Great Elm

Mells

Wadbury

Tedbury

Wadbury Valley

A

Fordbury Bottom

Murder Combe

B

Whatley Bottom

A The wooded Wadbury Valley conceals a former centre of industry. The stream provided water-power for fulling (cloth) mills since the 13th century, but for over one hundred years from 1744 it drove the Fussell edge-tool works. Scythes, reaphooks, spades and other agricultural implements were made here.

B The railway remains open for the quarry's freight traffic only.

DUNKERY BEACON
5.5 miles (8.9 km) Strenuous

Breathtaking views and magnificent scenery combine to make this an especially attractive walk. The high ground is windswept heather moorland, with the nature trail at the end of the walk going down sheltered valleys, where a mixed array of trees adds colour.

1 *Start from the National Trust car park at Webber's Post, which is 2 miles (3.2 km) south of Allerford Cross (see Walk **20** for details of buses). Cross the road and an open space to a second road. Turn right uphill along it.*

6 *Fork right to descend and bear left to the bottom of the valley. Turn left and cross the stream by a foot-bridge. Bear left and soon fork right uphill. Turn right at the top to return to Webber's Post car park.*

5 *Pass a farm and turn left to follow a signposted nature trail. Take the stile ahead then turn right, as signposted, over a second stile. Follow a fence and wall on your right. Continue through a gate and pass a path to Stoke Pero on your left. Fork left, as signposted.*

Cloutsham

Luccombe Hill

Dunkery Hill

Goosemoor Common

A Dunkery Beacon

519m

4 *Turn left, as signposted, for Stoke Ridge. Descend to cross a stream and turn sharply right up the path to a road, Go right along this and pass the road to Stoke Pero on your left.*

3 *Turn right along a downhill path. Reach a lower track.*

2 *Turn right along the track signposted 'To Dunkery Beacon'. Reach the summit cairn after 1 mile (1.6 km). Go ahead another 300 yards (275 m).*

A At 1704 feet (519 m), Dunkery Beacon is the highest point on Exmoor. Views extend to the hills above Abergavenny and Brown Willy in Cornwall. Beacons used to be lit here. Thomas Hardy wrote about a man living 'on Exon Wild by Dunkery Tor' in his poem *The Sacrilege*.

B The nature trail passes siver birch, oak and pine trees.

SELWORTHY

5 miles (8 km) Strenuous

0 ———————————— 1 mile
0 ———————————— 1 km

Splendid views can be enjoyed from this route, so come on a clear day if you can. Allow time to visit the beautiful model village of Selworthy, where the Information Centre is open *from Easter to late October (Mon-Sat* *10am-5pm, Sun 2-5pm).* There is a tea garden and National Trust shop.

4 *Turn left to enjoy a view over the coast near Porlock. Turn sharply right when you reach yellow-topped waymark posts.*

5 *Turn right at the next waymarked path junction and immediately fork left. Join the Coast Path and go right towards Minehead. Soon fork left and keep to the signposted Coast Path.*

6 *Leave the Coast Path by forking right to Selworthy Beacon. Go ahead to reach a road. Pass a track on your left, then bear right with a track signposted for Selworthy.*

3 *Fork right along the higher path, signposted to Hurlstone Point. This bears right around the tree-clad hillside to a small wooden gate. Go ahead through this and bear right up Lynch Combe, as signposted for Minehead. Reach a bench at a path junction.*

2 *Go up a lane and turn left at a signpost for Bossington. Cross a stile beside a gate and follow a fieldpath up to a kissing-gate in a hedge on your right. Continue through a gate into woodland. Take the track ahead and fork right to climb gradually to a bench at a path junction.*

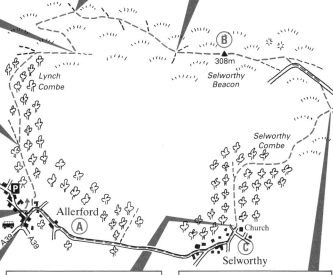

1 *Start from Allerford Cross, which is between Minehead and Porlock. This is served by Scarlet Coaches from both places, on a fairly frequent weekday basis (tel. 0643 704204 for timetable details). Motorists should park considerately nearby.*
Go into the village and take the packhorse bridge ahead over the river.

8 *Bear right at the road in Selworthy (passing the Information Centre on your right). Fork right along the lane for Allerford. This soon becomes a hedged track. Ignore the first lane on your left. Take the next lane back to the packhorse bridge. Return to the start.*

7 *Turn right at a crosstracks, as signposted for Selworthy. Descend to Selworthy Combe and follow the broad grassy track that swings left then right. Pass a plantation of conifer trees on your left, then go past broadleaved trees. Bear left to follow a stream on your right.*

A Allerford is an attractive village at a ford over the River Aller. Aller is probably derived from an old English word for alder tree. The packhorse bridge dates from about 1400.

B Selworthy Beacon is at 1012 feet (308 m) above sea level. As the view extends over the sea to South Wales, this is an impressive height. Dunkery Beacon can be seen on the other side.

C The village of Selworthy was a home for elderly estate workers in the 19th century. Now its cob walls, thatched roofs and gardens are in the care of the National Trust.

Walk 21

ALFOXTON

4 miles (6.4 km) Moderate

Follow in the footsteps of the poets on this walk. Samuel Taylor Coleridge persuaded William Wordsworth and his sister Dorothy to settle at Alfoxton for one year. They could not renew their lease because of local distrust. Their year here was memorable for the poets' rambles on these paths.

A This is Coleridge's 'roaring dell', which he often visited with Wordsworth. They represented the waterfall as a voice of nature.

B Alfoxton Park Hotel was built in 1710 as a mansion, by the St Albym family, who lived here from the 15th century to the early 1960s, when it became a hotel.

The Wordsworths were staying with Coleridge in nearby Nether Stowey in July 1797, when they stumbled upon Alfoxton whilst out walking. The last male heir had died in 1791 and his widow preferred to live elsewhere. The heir to the estate was still at school and the mansion was seldom occupied. The Wordsworths were able to rent the house for a year for only £23, from 14th July 1797. The housewarming dinner was on 23rd July, with John Thelwall (a renowned mob orator) and Coleridge as guests. Thelwall had spent time in the Tower of London in 1794 before being tried and acquitted on a charge of high treason. The locals concluded that Wordsworth must be a French spy. A government agent, James Walsh, was sent to spy on the future Poet Laureate. Walsh had a big nose and thought he had been found out when he heard Wordsworth and Coleridge talking about 'Spy Nozy'. It was, in fact, Spinoza they were discussing – a Dutch philosopher born of Jewish parents (1632-77).

Alfoxton

Over

0   1 mile

0   1 km

5   Continue down Hunts Lane, a hedged track. Fork left as indicated by a blue arrow on a waymark post. Walk above the stream on your right. Continue through a gate and along the right hand edge of a field, in a hollow below a hedge on your right.

6   Go ahead through a waymarked gate to walk with a fence on your left. Reach a junction with another bridleway and bear right through a waymarked gate. Go ahead to join a fence on your left and descend with it. Continue through a waymarked gate into woodland.

4   Go left down the lane, passing a riding centre on your left. Pass the access lane to a youth hostel on your right. Go ahead down Pardestone Lane to Kilve. Turn right along the A39, cross a bridge and go ahead for 400 yards (365 m).

7   Emerge through a gate into a field. Go ahead along the right hand edge and through a small wooden gate in the corner.
Continue beside the perimeter fence of woodland on your right.

8   Take the gate near a waymark post ahead. Follow a woodland path above the valley on your right. Reach a lane and go left along it back to the Plough Inn, Holford. Turn right for the bus stop.

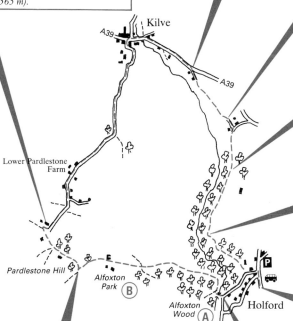

3   Turn sharply right at a hairpin bend. Climb through woodland and bear left. Fork right downhill with the lane at a junction with two tracks on your left. After passing the entrance to Lark Rise on your left, the surface deteriorates to a track. Descend and turn to a lane.

2   Turn right down the waymarked public footpath on your right. This is just after The Dye House. Go down steps to a foot-bridge over the waterfall, then go up steps on the other side of the valley to a lane. Turn right along it to pass Alfoxton Park Hotel on your left.

1   Start from the bus shelter in Holford, between Bridgwater and Watchet. Buses run to here from both places on Tuesdays and Fridays throughout the year and from Monday to Friday between Bridgwater and Woolacombe via Watchet, Minehead and Ilfracombe from late May to early October. For times tel 0823 255696. Cars may be parked considerably nearby.
Go right and pass the Plough Inn on your left. Turn left immediately after it along a lane which soon bears left.

MINEHEAD

2 miles (3.2 km) Strenuous

The old port of Minehead is at the foot of the steep hill which gave the town its name (from the Welsh 'mynydd').

This hill provides an initial test for South West Coast Path walkers as they start their long trek to Poole in Dorset.

There are excellent views of South Wales on a clear day.

4 *Fork right along the lowest of three paths ahead. Descend through woodland to a path junction. Turn sharply right to walk with the sea now on your left.*

3 *Follow the path as it zigzags uphill. At the top, turn right along a No Through Road, which is signposted as a public bridleway, to Greenaleigh Farm.*

1 *Start from Minehead railway station. Cars can be parked here, and buses stop nearby.*
Cross the road to the seafront and walk along it with the Bristol Channel on your right. As you approach the harbour, notice a sign saying 'Start of S. W. Coast Footpath to Poole (Dorset) 500 miles'.

5 *Go ahead along the road (Quay West), and go left to pass the harbour. Return along the seafront to the station.*

2 *Turn left across the road to take the path to North Hill, in between Woodcroft Cottage on your left and Seagate Cottage on your right. Go up steps and turn right with the signposted Coast Path. Pass an information board for this route. Climb steps in the top corner of this patch of woodland. Turn right along a higher path.*

Culver Cliff Wood · Lifeboat Station · Harbour · Minehead · Station

A The West Somerset Railway from Taunton terminated at Watchet at its opening in 1862, with the extension being completed by the Minehead Railway Company in 1874. British Rail closed the line in 1971, but local enthusiasm would not let it die, and on 26th March 1976, Lord Montague of Beaulieu flagged off the revived West Somerset Railway. This now has its eastern terminus at Bishop's Lydeard, where there is a bus connection with the main line at Taunton. Services, which are often steam-hauled, are seasonal. Tel 0643 821348 for details.

B The first sign for the South West Coast Path gives 500 miles (805 km) as the length of this national trail, while an information board along the way states 570 miles (917 km). The official guide book has it at 594 miles (965 km). Whatever the true distance, it is a tough one, best taken in short sections. This walk takes you on the first steps into Culver Cliff Wood. Backpackers usually cover the 21 miles (34 km) to Lynton on their first day. After North Devon, the path goes right around Cornwall to continue along the coast of South Devon. The final section takes in the cliffs of Dorset, to Poole.

C Daniel Defoe called Minehead the best port and safest harbour in Somerset. Built in 1601, it was enlarged in 1901. Herring used to be landed here and the import of coal and wool was also important. St Peter on the Quay church was once a coal and timber store. Robert Quirke donated it for use as a church in gratitude for being saved from a bad storm at sea. The Lifeboat Station stands as a reminder of such dangers. This was a select resort for the middle classes in the 19th century, and much of the town's wealth now comes from tourism. Butlins opened a holiday camp here in 1962.

Walk 23

DUNSTER

4 miles (6.4 km) Moderate

(scale bar: 0 — 1 mile / 0 — 1 km)

Dunster is a charming place, with a fine backcloth of attractive scenery. This northern edge of Exmoor has both broad-leaved trees and conifers, with open heathland giving splendid views. This walk can be linked with no **25** to form a route of 9 miles (14.5 km).

6 *Fork left and, after 50 yards (45 m), turn left along a path which climbs past trees to a waymark post.*

5 *Turn left at the track junction. Go uphill 30 yards (25 m), then turn sharply right uphill (as signposted for Alcombe). Follow this path as it turns left. Descend to a junction with a valley track. Go left along this and pass the access track to the youth hostel.*

4 *Take the gate ahead to enter woodland. Fork right onto the lower path. Emerge through a gate and walk with a wall on your right. Continue through a small wooden gate in the fence ahead. Descend to a gate in the next fence and turn right down a stony track, passing bracken on your left.*

(Map labels: Hagley; Alcombe Common; St Leonard's Well; Dunster; A396; Grabbist Hill; Castle; A396; P; and circled letters A, B, C, E, F)

3 *Take a kissing gate ahead and cross the field to another kissing gate in the wall ahead. Go through it to the old Butter Cross. Go left down St Georges Street for 100 yards (90 m). Turn sharply right along a hedged track.*

7 *Go ahead along the signposted path to Dunster, passing moorland on your right. Follow the red waymark posts. Pass a gate on your left up to a track junction. Turn left along the ridgeway near a National Trust sign on Grabbist Hill. Bear left, then fork right as waymarked in red. Descend through woodland and follow yellow waymarks down to a road. Go left back to Dunster.*

1 *Start from the Foresters Arms, at the corner of West Street and Park Street in Dunster. This is the terminus for the frequent weekday bus no 39 from Minehead. Cars may be parked considerably nearby.*
Go right along West Street and fork right to visit Dunster Castle.

2 *Continue up the High Street. Pass the Yarn Market at its top and, as the road turns right, go ahead up a narrow path (The Ball). Turn left along a road, but when it bends left, go straight ahead up a lane and through a wooden gate. Take the signposted path to the Buttercross and ignore a stile in the fence on your right.*

A Dunster Castle has been the home of the Luttrel family since Sir Hugh Luttrel bought it for 5000 marks (£3333) in 1376. The property is now in the care of the National Trust. It is *open Sat-Wed, Easter-Oct, 11am-5pm (noon-4pm Oct).* Admission charge.

B The Yarn Market dates from about 1600. Cloth was sold here.

C Notice Conygar Tower, an 18th-century folly.

D The Butter Cross was moved here from the market place in 1825.

E St Leonard's Well is housed in a small building on your left as you go up the hedged track.

F It was on Grabbist Hill, in 1848, that the hymn 'All Things Bright and Beautiful, All Creatures Great and Small' was composed by Cecil F. Alexander. Look out for kestrels, curlews and skylarks.

Walk 24
SEDGEMOOR
6 miles (9.7 km) Easy

Enjoy the most peaceful of walks along level paths above drainage ditches, where the Duke of Monmouth's rebellion against James II ended, at the Battle of Sedgemoor, in 1685. His brave Westcountrymen had to endure brutal reprisals after their defeat. Out of the tragedy has come a colourful painting above the door of the Sedgemoor Inn, depicting scenes from the battle and portraits of James II and the Duke of Monmouth.

A Westonzoyland's parish register records how the church was used after the Battle of Sedgemoor on 6th July 1685. 'The jniadgement (engagement) began between one and two of the clock in the morning. It continued near one hour and halfe. Their was kild upon the spott of the king's souldiers sixtenn, five of them buried in the church, the rest in church yeard . . . theire was kild of the rebils upon the spott about 300; hanged with us 22 . . . About 500 prisoners brought into our church, of which there was 79 wounded and 5 of them died of thire wounds in our church.' The wardens had to clean, fumigate and reglaze the church afterwards. The locals made the final total of corpses buried by them 1,384. They were the lucky ones, as Judge Jeffreys ordered about 300 more to be hanged, drawn and quartered, while about 800 were transported to the West Indies. Admire the elaborately painted sign above the door of the Sedgemoor Inn.

B James, Duke of Monmouth, was the eldest of Charles II's illegitimate sons. Born in Rotterdam in 1649, he was popular because he was a Protestant. Charles' brother, James the Duke of York, was the legitimate heir to the throne and succeeded in February 1685. He was a Roman Catholic. Many wished his illegitimate nephew could be king instead. So the Duke of Monmouth returned from exile in the Netherlands with just three ships and 80 men. Landing at Lyme Regis on 11th June 1685, he collected support as he marched towards Bristol. Most of the men who joined him were in their 30s or 40s and followed the Nonconformist trades, being carpenters, tailors, clothworkers and shopkeepers. They were against an autocratic, papist monarch. Over 7000 joined Monmouth, but the Duke had weapons for only 1500 of them – hence the term 'Pitchfork Rebellion'. A false report that the entire royal army was nearby led Monmouth (who failed to display much courage) to retreat from Keynsham. Back in Bridgwater, he learned that the royal army was at Westonzoyland. Expecting Monmouth to dig in at Bridgwater, the government troops had not entrenched their camp. Their tents were pitched behind the Bussex Rhine (now filled in - imagination is called for at the battle site). Seeing this through a spyglass from the tower of St Mary's Church, Bridgwater, Monmouth decided on a final, desperate gamble. He ordered a surprise night attack. In the event, the king's general, Feversham, had deployed troops against such a possibility, while the local cider wasn't allowed to affect them. Monmouth's local guide hesitated in the dark and an alert government sentry sounded the alarm. The rebels lost the vital crossing-point. Unable to cross Bussex Rhine in the dark, Monmouth's men fired futilely across it. Dawn showed how weak their position was. The Duke of Monmouth fled but was caught on 8th July. A week later he met death bravely at the hands of Jack Ketch, the executioner at Tower Hill.

C Rhines or rhynes (pronounced 'reen') are drainage channels. A widespread drainage system was first dug in the 13th century. King's Sedgemoor Drain was not cut until the 1790s. Farmers still adjust the water level so that rivers can flood the land with fertile silt. The willow trees that line the rhynes are pollarded to provide withies, or new shoots. These are slender and supple and used to make baskets. Look out for dragonflies in summer.

Over

0   1 mile

0   1 km

7   Go ahead over a foot-bridge and turn left, then right, to follow the hedge on your left. Turn left through a gate in the next corner. Go right along a hedged track to a road. Turn left into Westonzoyland and take Standards Road back to the inn.

6   Bear left at a fork and walk beside Moor Drove Rhyne. Pass under power lines and count the drainage ditches going off at right angles on your left. After the fifth, turn left through a waymarked gate.

5   Turn left to walk with King's Sedgemoor Drain on your right for nearly 2 miles (3.2 km). Cross a foot-bridge ahead over Chedzoy New Cut. Follow a track which eventually turns left.

4   Take the metal gate ahead and go through another at the next corner. Turn right along a track. Count the bridges over the drainage channel on your left, and turn left across the fourth bridge. Go ahead to the wide King's Sedgemoor Drain. Do not take the foot-bridge across it.

Chedzoy New Cut

Lang Moor

Battle of Sedgemoor
6th July 1685

King's Sedgemoor Drain

B

Bussex   Liney

A372

A Church
A372

C

Westonzoyland

P

1   Start from the Sedgemoor Inn at the centre of Westonzoyland, 3 miles (4.8 km) east of Bridgwater. There is a good bus service (Badgerline 158 and Southern National 16 Monday to Friday only) here from Bridgwater. The inn has a car park for patrons, while considerate roadside parking is possible nearby.
Go left and turn left down Church Lane.

2   Turn right at Monmouth Road and pass Sussex Square on your left. Go ahead to Bussex Farm, where signs invite you to divert left along a track for 250 yards (230 m) to the site of the Battle of Sedgemoor. Retrace your steps to the road, go across it and along Liney Road for 400 yards (365 m). Turn left down a private road, which is a public path, for 200 yards (185 m).

3   Turn left to cross the ditch and take a metal gate. Turn right immediately to walk parallel with the road. Take a metal gate ahead. Take the next metal gate on your right. This gives access to the road, where you go left. When the road bends right near a small brick shelter, bear left and keep above the drainage ditch on your left. Go ahead through a removable barbed wire fence. Cross the ditch on your left, then turn right to walk with it on your right. Go through a gateway and go left with another ditch on your left.

Walk 25
CARHAMPTON

5 miles (8 km) Moderate

Dramatic scenery provides excitement on this excursion, in an area associated with the legends of King Arthur. There is also the opportunity to visit a working water mill. The walk can be extended to 9 miles (14.5 km) by linking it with route no **23** at Dunster.

1 *Start from the Foresters Arms, at the corner of West Street and Park Street in Dunster, 2 miles (3.2 km) south-east of Minehead. This is the terminus for the frequent weekday bus* no 39 from Minehead. Cars may be parked considerably nearby. Go down Park Street towards Gallox Bridge. Divert left, then go right to see Dunster Working Water Mill.

Return to Park Street and resume your former direction. Cross the old packhorse bridge. Fork left to pass thatched cottages on your right.

Castle
Mill
Dunster
Gallox Bridge
Dunster Park
Carhampton Gate
Carhampton
Withycombe Hill Gate
Aller Hill
Withycombe Hill
Hill Lane
Withycombe Plantation

2 *Bear left at a waymark post to follow the red route to Carhampton. Cross a stile beside a gate and fork left immediately. Walk with a fence on your left and go through a kissing-gate ahead. Continue down a track to Carhampton.*

3 *Pass Winsors Lane on your left, then the High Street and The Crescent, both also on your left. Turn right at Hillview Road. Fork right up New Road. Bear left to a junction where you turn right. Pass Hill Lane on your left, then fork left as Meadowside goes to the right.*

4 *Pass an adventure playground on your right. Go ahead over a stile and bear left across a stile in the hedge. Cross a field diagonally to a stile giving access to Withycombe Lane. Go ahead for 30 yards (25 m).*

5 *Bear right up Hill Lane (a hedged track – ignore a lane going sharply right). Pass a hedged track on your right. Climb past trees to go ahead through a gate. Keep to the main track (do not turn right through a gate). Pass a forest on your right.*

7 *Bear left to descend with the red waymarked route. Turn right at a path junction. Go through a gate to return to your outward route. Turn left back to Dunster.*

6 *Follow the track through a red waymarked gate into the forest. Bear right for 30 yards (25 m), then fork left. Go right at a track to go through* a gate on your left. Go right down a red-waymarked track. Pass a path on your left, then fork left downhill.

A Dunster Working Water Mill is *open Apr-Oct, Sun-Fri (and Sat in Jul-Aug), 11am-7pm.* It stands on the site of a mill mentioned in the Domesday Survey of 1086.

B Carhampton was granted by King Arthur to St Carannog, who came here from Wales. The saint had a portable altar on which he floated, vowing to preach wherever it might land.

CLEEVE ABBEY

4 miles (6.4 km) Easy

This interesting walk can be reached by steam train. The route runs parallel to the West Somerset Railway, following a footpath on the course of the old West Somerset Mineral Railway. It then returns to Washford, where you can visit the ruins of a Cistercian Abbey and admire 13th- and 15th-century wall paintings.

5 *Turn left along the minor road for over 1 mile (1.6 km), ignoring all turnings. Go under a bridge which carries the railway. Continue past Castle Mead and Claydon Close on your right. Turn right at the A39 and almost immediately turn left to visit Cleeve Abbey, which is on your left. Return to the A39 and go left back to the station.*

1 *Start from Washford railway station. This is 5 miles (8 km) east of Minehead, from where there is also a bus service. Cars may be parked considerately in Washford.*

4 *Turn left to cross the railway, taking heed of a notice warning of trains. Take the path ahead, which runs in a hollow below a hedge on your left and woodland on your right. Continue over a stile beside a gate across your path. Reach a minor road.*

3 *Go ahead with the railway on your left for 1 mile (1.6 km). Ignore a gated crossing and a tunnel to Bye Farm on your left.*

2 *Go ahead across a road, passing a railway bridge on your left. Reach a school on your right and turn left along the track opposite. This soon bears right to a gate. Continue along the waymarked path across a playing field.*

Cleeve Priory

Bye Farm

Station

Washford

A39

Cleeve Abbey

A Washford Station was built in 1874, when the railway between Watchet and Minehead was opened. This was an extension to the West Somerset Railway, which branched off the main line west of Taunton in 1862. This is now a private steam railway. Their trains are not allowed to use British Rail's station at Taunton, so trains from Minehead terminate at Bishop's Lydeard. There is a bus service from there to Taunton station. Services are seasonal, tel: 0643 821348 for details.

B The West Somerset Mineral Railway was built to link the iron mines on Bredon Hill at Gupworthy with Watchet harbour. The ore was then shipped to smelters in South Wales. Opened in 1859, it was closed in 1898.

C Cleeve Abbey was founded for Cistercian monks at the end of the 12th century. Never one of the very prosperous monasteries, it does have an entire wall of one of the rooms covered by a 15th-century wall painting depicting St Catherine and St Margaret. There are also remains of 13th-century wall paintings. Dissolution came in 1536. The ruins are now in the care of English Heritage. Admission charge.

TAUNTON

4 miles (6.4 km) Moderate

Walk from the bustling centre of the county town of Somerset through a pleasant park and along waymarked paths to a vantage point on Cotlake Hill. Return along tracks, lanes and narrow paths to spend time in the County Museum, which is housed in the Great Hall of Taunton Castle.

A Taunton Castle can be dated from 1138, when Stephen and Matilda were waging their civil war. The King's half-brother was Henry of Blois, Bishop of Winchester. The manor of Taunton Deane was a great estate belonging to the Bishop of Winchester. Their interest began in the 8th century and by the end of the 11th it amounted to 43,000 acres. When Henry of Blois allied himself with Matilda, out of resentment at being overlooked for the post of Archbishop of Canterbury, he chose to erect a castle here. An earlier fortification had been built on an unknown site in Taunton in 710 by Ine, King of Wessex. His queen, Ethelburgh, had destroyed it in 722, possibly to prevent it falling into enemy hands.

The death of Stephen and the accession of Henry II led to Bishop Henry fleeing to France. His castle at Taunton was demolished in 1155, although some reconstruction took place when the bishop finally returned from exile. The Great Hall, which now houses the County Museum, was converted into a ground floor hall in 1246-7, when Bishop William Raleigh made other improvements. The date 1495 and the arms of Bishop Thomas Langton can be seen above the inner gateway. The castle seldom saw military action, but severe flooding in 1326 needed 2588 workmen to repair the damage.

The Pretender to the Tudor throne, Perkin Warbeck, passed this way with an army of 8000. Henry VII's forces easily overpowered them and the king came in person to interview the potential usurper. Nobody lost their head, but £441 was collected in fines. The same could not be said in 1685, when Judge Jeffreys held his 'Bloody Assizes' in the Great Hall. They started on 17th September and lasted for three days. On trial were members and suspected members of the Duke of Monmouth's army that lost to the forces of King James II at the Battle of Sedgemoor (see Walk **24**). 526 cases were dealt with: 19 were hanged, drawn and quartered; a further 139 were sentenced to the same fate, to be carried out in other towns and villages; and many were transported to work as slaves on sugar plantations in the West Indies. Jeffrey's ghost is said to haunt the place on every anniversary of the trials. Earlier, during the Civil War, the castle had seen action on behalf of Parliament. The town was besieged by Royalists in April 1645. A relief force arrived just in time and the siege was raised on 11th May. The anniversary was celebrated locally for long after.

Portraits of Judge Jeffreys and the Duke of Monmouth may be seen in the County Museum, which now occupies the Great Hall. There are also toys, dolls, animals and fossils on display. The Somerset Light Infantry collection includes the stars and stripes flag captured in the war between Britain and the USA in 1813. *Open 10am-5pm Mon-Sat (not Christmas and New Year).* Admission charge.

B Market House was built in 1772 to a design by Copleston Marre Bampfylde, an amateur. Opposite it is a timbered building erected by a Taunton merchant in the 14th century (but with frontage dating from 1578).

C Vivary Park's name refers to its former use as a vivarium or fishpond for the Bishops of Winchester. Today it offers all kinds of recreational opportunities for the townspeople, from feeding the ducks to playing bowls or golf. Note the memorial fountain.

D The Temple Methodist Church in Upper High Street, facing you as you emerge from the narrow path, is named after the Temple of the Muses. This was the name of a London book emporium owned by its founder, James Luckington. A Somerset man, he had risen from poverty to wealth. Returning to his native county and his old religion, he used his money to build The Temple for his fellow Methodists in 1809. They soon quarrelled with him and the upshot was that Luckington sold them The Temple in 1812 for £1050. This was less than half of the cost of its construction. Extended in 1846, it had school premises added in 1866. There are seats for over 1000 people.

Over

0 _____ 1 mile
0 _____ 1 km

1   Start from the Tourist Information Centre in Corporation Street, Taunton. This is near the bus station and car parks. Taunton also has a railway station.
    With your back to the library and Tourist Information Centre, cross the road and turn right. Go left up steps and along Castle Walk. Turn left past the Clarkes Tap Inn, then go right to the Castle Museum. Retrace your steps along Castle Walk and down the steps to Corporation Street.

8   Go ahead towards Wessex Road. This bears right. When it bends right again, turn left along a metalled footpath. Cross a foot-bridge and go right. Fork left along Cherry Tree Lane. Maintain this direction along paths and roads. Pass a car park, then bear right along a metalled path to Upper High Street. Turn right to the pelican crossing and go left back to the start.

7   Turn right along the track to pass Eastbrook Villa on your left. Continue beside a hedge on your right. Pass Haygrove Farm, away to your left. Take the gap in the hedge ahead. Walk with a hedge on your left through two fields. Cross a foot-bridge and reach Wyvern Road, Sherford.

2   Go left, then turn right across the road at the traffic lights. Pass Market House on your left. Go ahead along the pedestrianised High Street. Take the pelican crossing across Upper High Street ahead. Go through the gates into Vivary Park. Follow the signposted Poundisford Trail. Fork

Taunton

Wilton

Sherford

Haygrove Farm

Eastbrook

Vivary Park

Golf course

Sherford Bridge Farm

Cotlake Hill

left near the bandstand. Take the gate in the corner to a lane and turn right along it (signposted as the public footpath to Sherford). Follow this lane as it bends left to pass a cricket ground on your left and a children's playground on your right.

3   The lane deteriorates to a rough track past a golf course, and soon becomes an enclosed footpath above Sherford Stream, on your right. Go ahead over a stile and along the right hand edge of a field towards the distinct bump of Cotlake Hill.

4   Continue over a stile and along a concrete lane until it bends left. Go straight ahead across a waymarked stile and over a meadow to a stile in the hedge opposite. Follow the waymarked path between fields uphill to a stile in the top hedge. Go ahead over it and walk beside a hedge on your left. Take a gate in this to maintain your direction but with the hedge now on your right. Take the stile in the top corner to enter the plantation of trees on the summit of Cotlake Hill.

5   Cross another stile and bear right to a field. Turn left downhill, beside a hedge on your left.

6   Bear left through a waymarked gap in the hedge. Walk along the left hand edge of the field, and continue through a gate in the corner. Ignore steps descending to a stile on your left. Go ahead with the hedge on your left past another field and take the gap in the corner ahead to a track at Eastbrook.

MONTACUTE HOUSE

5 miles (8 km) Moderate

A visit to one of the most spectacular Elizabethan houses in the country is complemented by inspiring scenery on this walk. The view from the top of the folly on St Michael's Hill is memorable, and the woodland paths are enchanting. A fragment of the Holy Cross was reputedly found here during King Cnut's reign.

A Montacute House is an exceptional place. The house was completed in 1601 by Sir Edward Phelips. Lack of funds saved it from being altered over the centuries. When a new porch was added in 1786 it came from Clifton Maybank in Dorset, so it too was also Elizabethan. Things came to an end when mental instability became endemic within the family, with William Phelips (who died in 1889) becoming a compulsive gambler. The family finally left it in 1911. Lord Curzon rented it from 1915 and installed his mistress, the notorious authoress Elinor Glyn.
Of her it was said:
'Would you like to sin
with Elinor Glyn
on a tiger skin?'
When the National Trust acquired the place in 1931, it was bare. The solution has been to make the Long Gallery an outstation of the National Portrait Gallery. Thomas Hardy called the place 'Montislope' in *The Mayor of Casterbridge*. The house is *open Apr-Oct, noon-5.30pm, Wed-Mon*. Admission charge.

B This is the site of the deserted medieval hamlet of Witcombe.

C Hamdon Hillfort is one of the largest (in area) in Britain. It was occupied from Neolithic to Roman times. Quarries here provided honey-coloured limestone for Exeter Cathedral.

D St Michael's Hill is the 'mons acutus' (steep hill) which gave Montacute its name. When the Normans built a castle here, it provoked an English uprising in 1068. This was especially holy ground, reputedly being where a fragment of the holy cross was discovered.

Montacute House

Over

0   1 mile

0   1 km

6 *Bear right with the waymarked footpath along the tree-clad ramparts. Go through a gap in the wall on your left and bear right. Eventually cross a stile in a fence on your right. Turn left along the woodland path for 400 yards (365 m) and go ahead over a stile. Fork right to emerge from the wood.*

7 *Bear left across a field. Turn right over a stile beside a gate and a National Trust sign, to enter the woodland of St Michael's Hill. Take the gravel path which spirals to the folly at the summit. Retrace your steps to the field. Turn right to follow the fence on your right.*

8 *When you are level with another stile in the fence on your right, turn left downhill. Go through a kissing-gate beside a signpost. Descend to take a kissing-gate in the lower fence. Turn right to pass playing fields on your left. Reach a road (Bishopston). Turn right and then go left down Middle Street back to The Borough.*

1 *Montacute is 4 miles (6.4 km) west of Yeovil. Start from the square known as The Borough in Montacute. Cars may be parked here. Buses come from Yeovil – tel 0460 40309 for times.*
Face the Phelips Arms and go left for the entrance to Montacute House. Continue along Middle Street. Turn left when facing the King's Arms Inn. This No Through Road becomes a public bridleway. Pass a duck pond on your left and go ahead to Hollow Lane.

2 *Go right along Hollow Lane for 20 yards (18 m), then turn right over a stile. Turn left immediately to follow the fence on your left. Go ahead over two stiles, then cross a stile beside a gate on your left to reach a road junction.*

3 *Turn right for 10 yards (9 m), then turn left across the road to the hedged track waymarked as the public footpath to Witcombe. Follow this as it turns right to a stile beside a gate. Bear left over this to go down a grass track to the bottom of the valley. Go ahead over a stile, and continue across a stile at the far end of the valley.*

4 *Turn sharply right up an old green lane. Bear right at a fork to keep just inside the right hand edge of woodland. Pass another waymarked path bearing left. Go ahead through the rampart of Hamdon Hillfort to emerge over a stile. Turn right and follow the hedge on your right.*

5 *Reach a road and go left along it for 300 yards (275 m). Turn right at a waymarked post and follow the public footpath towards Montacute.*

CADBURY CASTLE

6 miles (9.7 km) Moderate

Cadbury Castle has, for many visitors, a truly magical atmosphere. Local legend states that if you chanced to come at full moon on a midsummer night you will see King Arthur's knights ride again. The site is recognised by many as being the castle of Camelot.

A Corton Denham's church is dedicated to St Andrew and was founded in 1267.

B Corton Ridge provides splendid views across the Somerset Levels to the Quantocks.

C John Leland wrote in 1542:
'At the very South Ende of the Church of South Cadbyri stanithe Camalotte, sumtyme a famose Town of Castell. Much Gold, Sylver and Coper of the Romaine Coynes hathe been found there yn plowing; and lykewise in the fields, in the rootes of this Hille, with many other antique things and especial by Eeste. Ther was found in hominum memorium a Horse Shoe of Sylver at Camalotte. The people can tell nothing ther, but they have herd say that Arture much resortid to Camalat'.

Cadbury Castle is, indeed, the best-known of the reputed sites of King Arthur's Camelot. Don't expect stone towers, of course – this is an ancient hillfort. Dating from at least 3000BC, it was expanded in the Iron Age, in time to serve as a defence against the Romans. The future emperor Vespasian was probably the Roman commander who took the hillfort in AD43. It must have been a fierce fight because the remains of at least 30 people killed in his attack have been uncovered at just one of the entrances. The Romans later broke down the defensive wall about AD70. These facts emerged during excavations here between 1966 and 1970. These were carried out because of the hillfort's later associations with King Arthur, and are described by L. Alcock in his book *By South Cadbury is that Camelot.* Alcock found evidence for the hillfort having been re-occupied by a King Arthur-type figure around the most likely time (from about 500). The refortification was on a massive scale. The evidence uncovered included a large timber hall built in the post Roman period in Celtic style. It was in the centre of the plateau, at a spot known since at least the 16th century as the site of Arthur's Palace.

Guarding the south-western approach to the hall are the remains of a gatehouse. Surrounding the entire perimeter for some three-quarters of a mile (1.2 km), surmounting the old earthen ramparts, was a wall of the same period, 16 feet (4.9 m) thick, built in stone with wooden beams. Artefacts found include fragments of wine and oil jars imported from the eastern Mediterranean around 500, and similar to others found at Tintagel (the legendary birthplace of Arthur in Cornwall). On the earthworks at the south-eastern corner of Cadbury the excavators found the remains of a young man thrust head downward into a pit – a foundation sacrifice.

Legend tells how the young Merlin was intended to be such a sacrifice.

From a height of 500 feet (150 m), there is an uninterrupted view of Glastonbury Tor and of Brent Knoll. Beacon fires could have linked it easily with the Bristol Channel and King Arthur's heartland of Gwent and Glamorgan. South Cadbury was most likely a vital and impressive fortress near the border between Arthur's territory and that of the mysterious Gewissae, the so-called 'West Saxons', whose leaders had Celtic names, probably shared the same Gnostic brand of Christianity as Arthur and, at least initially, seemed to be allies of Arthur, rather than Saxon invaders. They inhabited Dorset, just to the south of Cadbury Castle, where Arthur exercised no authority.

There is a legend that King Arthur and his knights sleep inside this hollow hill. Every seven years, on St John's Eve (23rd June), they ride out along a causeway which used to exist between the villages of North Barrow and South Barrow, towards Glastonbury. A true-hearted person who bathes his or her eyes in Arthur's Well on the fourth fosse (trench) of the fort's eastern slope can see the magical sight. Others can just hear the jingle of bridles.

Over

CADBURY CASTLE

Continued

5 Turn left up a track marked 'Castle Lane leading to Camelot Fort'. Explore the hillfort and go back to the road. Go left to the church of St Thomas á Becket.

6 Retrace your steps from the church, passing Castle Lane on your right. Look out for Crangs Lane on your left. 100 yards (90 m) after it, turn left over a stile to take the waymarked public footpath towards Sigwells. Cross the field to a waymarked foot-bridge.

7 Cross the foot-bridge and go along the left hand edge of the next field. Take the green lane ahead for 20 yards (18 m), then turn right through a gateway. Turn left immediately to walk with the hedge on your left. Continue through a small metal gate in the corner and along the top of the next field. Whitcombe Farm is on your right.

4 Turn right at a T junction. Bear left with the road and pass Crangs Lane on your right.

3 Near the foot of the hill, go through a small metal gate. Take a tree-lined path to a road. Go left and then immediately turn right to cross the road at a junction. Follow the road signposted to South Cadbury.

2 When the track divides, take the right hand gate ahead and turn right to walk along the ridge. Keep the fence on your right and go ahead over stiles for three-quarters of a mile (1.2 km). Go ahead through a waymarked gate and follow the path as it bears right down the side of Parrock Hill.

8 Turn right along a path, which becomes a green lane. Bear left to pass a farm building on your right. Go through a gate, across a farmyard, and along a lane to a road. Go left, pass another road on your left and go ahead 100 yards (90 m).

9 Climb steps to a stile on your left. Bear right to go above a hedge and turn right to follow it. Go above a gate in a recessed corner ahead. Continue to a green lane which descends to the road. Turn left along this back to the start.

1 Start from the Post Office at Corton Denham. This village is 4 miles (6.4 km) north of Sherborne, off the B3145. Cars can be parked considerately. There is a bus service (no 19) provided on Wednesdays and Fridays by Wakes Services, tel 0963 33124, from Bruton (on British Rail's Bristol to Weymouth line). Go left to pass the telephone box and take the road out of the village. Turn left down a No Through Road (Ridge Lane). This becomes a grass track.

Map labels: Cadbury Castle, Church, South Cadbury, Eastcombe Farm, Charwell Field, Stonehill, Parrock Hill, The Beacon, Corton Ridge, Corton Denham, Church

DUNDON

4.5 miles (7.2 km) Moderate

0   1 mile

0   1 km

This is a very special walk, more than just a pleasant ramble along fieldpaths, through woodland and down hedged tracks. This ground is within the famous Glastonbury Zodiac, where huge landscape figures are marked out by natural and artificial features. Recorded throughout history, it is best explained by Mary Caine's book *The Glastonbury Zodiac*, which also contains an illuminating aerial photograph.

6 *Descend to a fixed gate with a stile in it. Cross this to take a hedged track. Just after this turns to the right, turn left down a narrow, enclosed, path to the road in Dundon. Go left and soon fork right to pass a school. Go ahead along a track, and continue along the left hand edges of two fields. In the third field reach a gate on your left. Take it to retrace your steps back to the start.*

2 *Turn left at a waymark post for a public footpath to Littleton. This goes between two houses to a fieldgate. Go through it and bear left across the corner of a field, then walk beside a hedge on your left to a gate in the corner. Continue with a hedge on your left around the edge of the next field, to a stile.*

1 *Start from the slightly staggered crossroads in the centre of Compton Dundon, 2 miles (3.2 km) south of Street. Bus no 376 stops nearby. Head for Ham Lane where careful roadside parking is possible.*
Go down Ham lane for 250 yards (230 m).

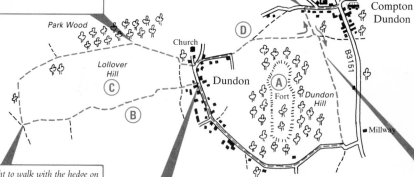

5 *Turn right to walk with the hedge on your right. Maintain your direction through a gate in the corner, but with the hedge now on your left. Remain in this field by turning right in the next corner and climbing with the hedge still on your left. Take a small wooden gate in the top corner. Pass a stile on your left and climb to go ahead through a gate in the top corner.*

4 *Turn left along a lane, which passes Lockyer's Farm on your left and continues as a hedged track. Pass another hedged track going right. Go ahead and come to a corner where the track turns left with the hedge. Go straight ahead through a gate to climb gradually up a field. Take a gate in the far hedge.*

3 *Continue beside the hedge on your left, then go through a gate in the corner ahead. Keep the hedge on your left as you maintain this direction through a small metal gate in the next corner. Reach a minor road and turn right along it towards Dundon. Pass Hayes Lane on your left. Go ahead another 300 yards (275 m).*

A Dundon Hill, when viewed from above, is shaped like the head of Jesus, the heavenly twin of the Zodiac. It points west, with north at the top. Dundon means the 'fort of wisdom'. It is crowned by a beacon tumulus.

B This track forms part of the Somerset Way, 63 miles (101 km) from its finish in Bath.

C Ancient lynchets on Lollover Hill supposedly mark Jesus' ribs in the pattern of the Zodiac.

D This footpath helps to outline the raised arm of Jesus in the Zodiac figure.